SELF-TALK
at
WORK

Business Success Enabled by
Enlightened THINKING

What are
<u>YOU</u>
THINKING?

A sequel to
CHARACTER Plus COMMON SENSE

Richard Sevcik

Contents

The Challenge of Leadership

⸺ ∞ ⸺

We are continually 'talking' to ourselves within our minds, within our brain cells. I do it, you do it, we all do it! In fact you are doing it right now. Maybe you're even thinking that I'm a bit crazy. But, if I'm correct, you are 'talking' to yourself about me right now. We are often inclined to dismiss this self-talk as just passing the time of day, and as being rather unimportant. But, self-talk is not just idle chatter in our minds. Your self-talk can and will shape your personality, and eventually determine your behavior!

Nearly 40 years ago I read the book *I'm OK, You're OK* by Thomas A. Harris, M.D. Ever since then, I have been intrigued by the impact of my own self-talk on my life. I've read many books that have dealt with this topic. But, I've never read a book that deals with self-talk in the context of a work environment. So, I've decided to write this book on exactly that topic. In my first book, *Character Plus Common Sense*, I identified 10 key principles that are necessary for success in the work environment. This new book will propose the best possible self-talk, or *Enlightened Thinking*, to enable each of these 10 principles in our lives.

I believe that it's useful to identify common negative self-talk, or *Stinking Thinking*, that often surrounds our thinking concerning each of these 10 principles. You may even recognize some of these Stinking Thinking phrases in your own self-talk.

Unfortunately, I have observed that in most cases, our minds are often filled with negative self-talk. We need to be aware of these bad habits and purposefully replace negative thinking with constructive thinking. This is my main objective in writing this book: I would like to help you think 'right' and as a result, be successful. Or in other words, this book is all about your thought life and how it impacts your actions.

So, please explore with me 'how' you are currently practicing self-talk as it applies to your job and your life. We will together consider our thinking habits. We will become conscious of how our minds function in different situations. And, let's see if we can develop much better thinking habits that can lead to a higher likelihood of success and happiness.

As you read this book you may be wondering, does this approach to self-talk for these 10 principles of success really work? I believe that based upon my experience, the answer is clearly "yes." I began to apply these principles at Hewlett-Packard (HP) during the early 1990s. Our computing business grew at a most impressive rate.

Later, I joined Xilinx, Inc. in 1997. At that time the annual revenue at Xilinx totaled $560 million. By the year 2006, the Xilinx annual revenue had increased to $1.7 billion with a net income in excess of 25 percent. This growth rate and profitability were, and are, world class. As a result of this success, the Xilinx market capitalization increased from $2.4 billion in 1997 to $8 billion in 2006. In addition to these wonderful financial results, Xilinx was also ranked among the *Fortune* magazine annual list of the "Top 10 Best Companies to Work For" for four consecutive years. I'm still amazed that we were able to accomplish such an awesome feat.

These accomplishments were the result of a great team of people working together toward common goals. And, we had jointly developed an excellent culture based upon these 10 principles of success, upheld by positive self-talk. Our team employed a can-do attitude with mutual support for each other and for the company's goals.

By the way, if you are curious, in the appendix in the back of this book you can read an explanation of the Biblical basis for these 10 key principles. As a Christian I find it very reassuring that God has revealed these principles to us for our guidance. God wants us to be a success in all that we do on this earth. And amazingly, God has a lot to say to us about our self-talk as well. The Bible explains that as we think, so we are. God really does want us to be successful!

I would encourage everyone to read the appendix. If you are unfamiliar with the Bible, I think you will find the appendix instructive. It's not an accident that I read the book *I'm OK, You're OK* 40 years ago. I believe that God led me to the class where the book was being taught.

My youngest daughter was in need of excellent day care. In our neighborhood, the best day care was offered at a local Bible-based Church, and they required that the parents attend one of their adult classes. Coincidently this was the only class offered on the evening that I was available. It was a great class taught by their Senior Pastor. He changed my life forever. Or, I should say that he and God changed my life forever!

Finally I would like to thank the numerous people who 'adopted' me during my 40 year career. They were my mentors. They cared about me - really cared! I would encourage each of you to look for someone in your life who is wiser than yourself, and ask them to 'adopt' you. Ask them to give you wise advice that you can embrace with open arms.

Numerous people have helped me in the final editing of this book. I would especially like to thank Mark van Wyk, and William P. Parkhurst. All of the profits from this book will be donated to several charities. They each provide help to disadvantaged people all across the United States and around the world.

As I write this book I would like to once again (it's my second book) thank my wife, Charlene, who has been very patient with me. At times, I really think that she is an angel whom God placed in my life.

Introduction

Self-Talk
&
Key Principles of Success

— ⊱≋⊰ —

My main objective in writing this book is to present pro-active techniques that enable positive self-talk in the context of key principles for success in your work environment. My first book presented five key management principles:

➤ Be Aggressive - Take Smart Risks
➤ Keep It Simple - As Simple As Possible
➤ Focus - And Focus Again
➤ Measure It - Or Don't Do It
➤ A Company Is Only As Good As The People.

In this second book, I will further explore how we need to think about these principles in order to effectively implement them in a work environment. We are always 'talking' to ourselves in our minds as we go through a typical day. This private, in-our-mind talking, is often referred to as *self-talk*.

We often think that this idle self-talk is meaningless and harmless. But, how we think influences our attitude about everything; and, as a result our self-talk will eventually determine our behavior. We can and must consciously control this self-talk in order to be successful.

We need to replace destructive self-talk with constructive self-talk.

Controlling self-talk sounds pretty simple, but it is difficult to accomplish on a daily basis. Very often experiences in our lives, and in particular in our childhood, have preprogrammed us to dwell upon certain destructive self-talk patterns or habits. The only way to improve our results at work is to grow on a personal basis. There can be personal growth but only if we change. We must change our behavior.

The key to changing our behavior is changing our self-talk.

That's what this book is all about.

As I presented in my first book, even when applying these five key management principles, the fact is that not everyone possesses the personality traits to be a successful manager or leader. People management does require a certain set of character traits. These traits can be developed if you put your mind to the task.

Your self-talk has a huge impact on your personality. Our personalities are not cast in stone! Once again change is possible as we learn to control our self-talk. I believe that these five character traits are also critical to success; so I will discuss each of these character traits in the first five chapters of the book. These traits are:

➤ Integrity – Be Honest
➤ Humility – Focus On Others
➤ Joyfulness – Enjoy Life
➤ Openness – You Can't Hide
➤ Trust – Be Faithful.

In order to effectively develop these character traits I will also explore the self-talk that surrounds these behaviors, just as I propose to do with the five key management principles.

I have devoted one chapter to each of these 10 concepts —five management principles plus five character traits— which help develop successful leadership qualities. Of course these concepts do not each stand alone. They must be practiced in an integrated fashion.

Success depends upon the leverage that these concepts gain from each other. In fact, I believe that if one principle is practiced to the extreme, without balance from the others, success will be lacking. I have included a one-page depiction of these principles of success at the end of this Introduction as a visual reminder of all 10 concepts presented in this book. I have also included a one-page depiction of the process of self-talk as a visual reminder of how to optimize your thinking.

I wrote these books because after thirty years of management experience, I have come to believe that successful management is both simple (not complicated) and difficult (not easy). Management is simple because there are only a few, in my opinion 10, common sense management concepts that must be mastered on the job. But, management is also difficult because by human nature, we all tend to get distracted from these key concepts.

Maybe it's because deep down inside we all tend to be a bit lazy. But in addition, I think we all tend to want to be inventive as we go along in our daily lives. During a typical day at work, rather than follow principles, we want to get creative. Our self-talk often pushes us to try something new. We may not feel like following company procedures. To be sure, creativity has its place at work, but it should not distract us from key fundamental principles.

Excellence in management does require a great deal of focus to details to be successful. Focus is a habit that is not often taught in our society. We often want to be free to do our own thing. And, people think that they can do multiple things at the same time. We may be tempted to surf on the internet while speaking with someone or to check email while attending a family gathering. In addition, at work we can be repeatedly distracted by urgent interruptions. Nearly everybody and everything wants our attention - now. But we can't let these interruptions dominate our work day. We must set time aside to complete the work dictated by these key management concepts.

Success is really all about personal focus. It's all about how we think, which leads to how we act (and in many cases how we do not take action).

Excellence in management requires us to have the focus to manage our own creative distractions, and we must manage the external interruptions as well. These are two of the key reasons why management is difficult.

By the way, as you consider these leadership principles for yourself, be mindful of those who work with you in your group. It would be wise to expect them to practice these principles as well. In fact when hiring someone, these principles could be a checklist for evaluating different candidates.

FIVE CHARACTER TRAITS

You may be wondering why I believe that these character traits are also critical to success. Since all workers are human, there are style traits that I believe can impact your management results in a very significant way. We humans are emotional creatures. For example people can be attracted to you, or, they can be repulsed by your style.

These style traits, or key character traits, are: integrity, humility, joyfulness, openness, and trust. I believe that the more you can demonstrate these traits to fellow workers, the more likely it is that they will be attracted to you as a manager and a leader. And, if they like you, they will usually be motivated to let you lead them. They will give you grace, instead of criticism. They will be attracted to your leadership.

It is most important that you realize that these character traits can't be faked. You either have integrity or you don't. In a recent *Forbes* magazine article, publisher Rich Karlgaard wrote: "God and the tweeters will strike down those who fake it."[1] Open communication is now the norm in our society. Don't try to fool fellow workers on these traits. It just will not work. In fact it will cause people to disdain you, making your management success nearly impossible.

I've devoted an entire chapter, Chapter One, to the topic of integrity. I hesitate to call this a 'style' issue, but it's not a management principle either. Maybe, it's best thought of as a life principle, or simply a crucial character trait. Chapter One in many ways is the most critical chapter in this book. Integrity as a manager enables everything!

I believe that the great failing that we are experiencing today in government and financial institutions is due to a lack of integrity. It seems as though every day, the internet headlines are pointing out another high profile leader in America who has had a failing of integrity. A leader cheats and then tries to defend themself, usually not fooling anyone but themself.

It's very interesting that in 1963 Martin Luther King Jr. said that he looked forward to a day when people will "...

not be judged by the color of their skin, but by the content of their character." Now in 2012, after much progress has been made concerning racism, character is the trait that is sorely lacking. During these nearly five decades, it seems as though we have lost the characteristic that Dr. King was holding in highest esteem: integrity. Maybe we as a society must relearn that after all is said and done, honesty is the best policy.

If people can't believe you, they will not follow you.

Why should they? Think about it!

WHAT IS SUCCESS?

I think that at the outset of this book it is appropriate for me to define success. There are of course many ways to think about success. Most people today would define it as the attainment of wealth, and the prestige and power that often accompanies wealth. However, very often, the wealthy are not happy. In fact the wealthy tend to have the highest suicide rate in America. Success in life is a very deep subject. But for the purposes of this book, with its focus on management, I will define success as the achievement of your business goals. I would however encourage you to set goals that will bring you prosperity, peace, and joy.

In a workplace context we are tempted to only focus on completing a successful project. But, your goals should also include goodwill for your team members. As I have grown older I have realized that successful projects come and go, but it's the people that are truly valuable. If your goals as a manager include the growth of your team members, then you can expect many, many successful projects.

JUST THINKING?

Self-talk is the most powerful force in our lives. We must learn to control our thinking. This is a huge challenge because our thoughts can be manipulated by our emotions, by other people in our presence, and certainly by our childhood experiences.

If you are a sports fan let me give you an impactful example. I really enjoy watching the San Francisco 49ers football team. When they win my thoughts are usually positive. When they lose I can spend a lot of self-talk in negative circular patterns. Unfortunately these thoughts are not only about the 49ers; they can impact other aspects of my life as well. For example, I can become easily irritated at home. That doesn't make sense (it's only a game) but it is a natural human reaction. Our emotional state of mind has an impact on our thought patterns. Soccer fans throughout the world will even riot on occasion, killing people, when their team loses.

If you are a stock market enthusiast, let me give you another example. How do you react when a stock that you have invested in has a significant drop in value? Are you inclined to get frustrated or frightened and decide to sell the stock at the low price? It is well known that feelings have a strong influence over our buy and sell decisions.[2] We must be aware of these emotionally triggered self-talk patterns and resulting behaviors. We must learn to stop reacting illogically.

Before making decisions we need to think. In fact we need to think about our thinking in advance of that circumstance!

We also need to think in advance about our feelings. Our feelings actually exist in our brain. Many people vaguely assign feelings to their heart organ. We have probably all heard someone say something like: "My heart aches for my mom." But I think we all know that the human heart organ does not have feelings. Sometimes I think people refer to their "heart-felt feelings" as an excuse to let their feelings be out of their rational control. But, we can control our feelings.

Feelings are an activity of our brain cells. We can control these thoughts.

We must ask ourselves who or what is in control of our thinking and of our lives? Is it the 49ers or the stock market?

This is your life; think about it. Is it the chemistry of reactive emotions that control your actions, like with a football game? Or, are your actions controlled by your values, logic, and reason? We must be self-aware of how we think.

Personally there are times when I can almost 'hear' my self-talk. I can actually catch myself thinking about my thinking. (This of course means that I am thinking about my thinking about my thinking.) These self-talk dynamics will have an impact on every aspect of our lives: family relationships, leisure activities, and work.

For the purposes of this book I will focus on self-talk at work. We must learn to effectively and proactively use our brains while we are at work in order to optimize our success. As we explore the concept of self-talk at work I will repeatedly discuss a process of self-talk which can help control our thinking and our behavior.

Let's begin by focusing on the concept of the *Big Decision*, as I will refer to it.

I would encourage you to seriously think about how you would prefer to behave in a given situation, well ahead of the occurrence of that situation.

You should strive to make the Big Decision about that behavior while you are in a thoughtful state of mind and not in a reactive state of mind. We not only must be fully aware of our thought processes, but we must also learn to control our thoughts through advanced planning. Our behavior is the result of our thinking both at the instant of our behavior, and also as a result of the environment in our minds created by our earlier thoughts. We need to mentally turn on positive thinking (Enlightened Thinking) and therefore turn off negative thinking (Stinking Thinking).

For example you may frequently find yourself thinking "I am stupid." Or maybe in your case you think that you are smarter than everyone else. We humans do tend to view ourselves in the extremes. We also tend to believe that we are more objective than we really are; so we actually believe that our thinking is truth. We must first of all become aware of these thoughts. We can't let our minds, which have been molded by such factors as our childhood and interactions with our close friends, 'speak' to us in an uncontrolled fashion.

We need to be aware of our self-talk.

We must ask ourselves if our self-talk is indeed accurate. And most important, we must learn to control our thinking by *Advanced Thought Planning*, as I will refer to it. During a time of quality thoughtfulness, that is, during a time of clear and deep thinking, we need to analyze our thoughts. For example through Advanced Thought Planning we need to determine if in reality "I am stupid" is an accurate thought. Or more likely, we can determine that this incorrect self-assessment is the result of a parent who unfairly and habitually vented their own poor self-image upon us.

Through Advanced Thought Planning I can decide that I am not stupid, and that I will not allow those thoughts to occupy my mind. I must then make the Big Decision: I am not stupid. Furthermore I must plan on how I will displace the Stinking Thinking, "I am stupid," with Enlightened Thinking, "I am very intelligent."

This Big Decision will allow you to stop the frequent negative self-talk that disempowers you periodically during the course of a day. If you are someone who thinks that you are smarter than everyone else, then you should realize that your resulting arrogance is turning off your coworkers. You should also objectively realize that there must be some people smarter than you. I'm sure you can think of someone you know with more intelligence than you. If not, you need to find some new friends.

You need to construct a plan through Advanced Thought Planning that enables you to replace the Stinking Thinking with Enlightened Thinking, thereby empowering yourself to success through your Big Decision and the resulting positive action.

The plan that I recommend to maximize your Enlightened Thinking is simple. As a result of your Big Decision, write down your specific desired Enlightened Thinking on a piece of paper and carry it with you as often as possible. Memorize what is written on that piece of paper. Use your Enlightened Thinking as your smartphone banner and as your laptop screen saver. Totally immerse yourself in this positive self-talk for 60 days. Then every time that your mind wanders to the associated Stinking Thinking, immediately repeat your Enlightened Thinking three times to yourself. You can't stop thinking about Stinking Thinking unless you replace it with something better. Our minds usually require some occupying thought. The best approach is to replace Stinking Thinking with Enlightened Thinking. You must mentally turn off the former and turn on the latter. It takes about two months to create this new mental thought pattern, but it can be done. Just think about it: in only two months you can change the rest of your life!

I have found that it is usually possible to control my feelings in any situation. Through Advanced Thought Planning I have made the Big Decision that I will be joyful. When I find my mind occupied by fear or sadness that is inappropriate, when I engage in Stinking Thinking, I purposefully switch to Enlightened Thinking. I will recall joyful memories, or play a favorite song in my mind, or take the time to watch a comedy show on television. By controlling my self-talk, it's amazing how quickly I can change my thought pattern and feelings toward a positive direction.

Throughout this book, for each of the 10 principles of success, I will give suggested examples of Enlightened Thinking that you may want to practice. However I think that you will find that you can only focus on one aspect of Enlightened Thinking at a time. After that one topic is mastered in 60 days, you can then move on to another, and then another. This approach is a simple process to form positive habits in your self-talk. This method of purposeful thinking should be a lifelong pursuit!

At the end of each chapter I have included a section entitled "Personal Application." These questions are intended to help you apply the contents of the chapter to your work life. Hopefully, you will seriously think about taking action to build new, successful self-talk habits which will lead you to positive results in your career.

THE WRAP-UP

Finally, I use the word 'manager' frequently in this book in the context of a manager in the workplace. But, the principles presented in this book are applicable to any role of leadership. A leader is simply someone who strongly influences other people or events. You may be the leader of your family or the leader of your baseball team; and you will find these principles very useful. Or, as an employee with no direct people management responsibilities, you should consider yourself as a leader. Your employer is paying you to get a job done. As a leader you should determine the most effective way for your employer to get a great return on their investment in you. If you do that well, you will soon receive recognition and reward for your leadership. This is of course is a great example of Enlightened Thinking!

For the purpose of clarity, here is a simple summary of this entire book.

> ➢ Always live and work with integrity; be honest with yourself and all the people that you impact on a daily basis.
> ➢ Keep in mind that your character is on display at all times.
> ➢ Be intelligently aggressive in everything you do; remember that without risk there is usually little to gain.
> ➢ Always keep your products and your organization as simple as possible; it really does make life easier to live.
> ➢ Focus is crucial to getting things done quickly and successfully; it's often necessary to say "no" to a myriad of distractions.

➤ In business and in life set goals that are measurable, so you can know for sure that you are making progress.

➤ Always remember that people are your company's most valuable resource; and, that definitely includes you!

➤ Be aware of your self-talk. Strive to accomplish Enlightened Thinking throughout the entire day by practicing Advanced Thought Planning.

➤ For each of these 10 principles, make the Big Decision that will empower you to success.

PRINCIPLES OF SUCCESS

— — — SUCCESS — — —

FOCUS

BE AGGRESSIVE

KEEP IT SIMPLE PLEASE

MEASURE IT — — OR DON'T DO IT

A COMPANY IS AS GOOD AS THE PEOPLE

— — — — — — — — — — — — — — — — — — — —

INTEGRITY * TRUST * HUMILITY

OPENNESS * JOYFULNESS

PROCESS OF SELF-TALK

— — — SUCCESS — — —

THE BIG DECISION

ENLIGHTENED THINKING

ADVANCED THOUGHT PLANNING

— — — — — — — — — — — — — — — — —

PURPOSEFULLY TURN ON & TURN OFF

CHOSEN THOUGHTS

Chapter One

Integrity - Be Honest

―≈≈≈―

KEY POINT:
Always live and work with integrity; be honest with yourself and with all the people that you impact on a daily basis.

STINKING THINKING:
Everyone else is exaggerating, so to get ahead I need to exaggerate too. No one will know.

ENLIGHTENED THINKING:
I will be strong and successful by being honest in all my actions.

Integrity is simply being honest. Say what you mean and mean what you say! Do what you say you will do. And, always be sure to speak what is on your heart with compassion.

People are attracted to leaders who are sincere and do what they promise. Unfortunately, it's become commonplace in our society to spin the truth to one's own convenience. Saying different things to different audiences in order to please people just doesn't work. That will not bring lasting happiness. That is the result of Stinking Thinking. People will eventually figure you out, and when they do, they will definitely not be happy with your lying. Politicians today seem to be learning this lesson the hard way, as evidenced by the current unpopularity of the United States Congress.

What makes us think that we can or should lie? What causes us to think that we will succeed if we lie? I believe that it has a lot to do with our self-talk. If we set up a mental attitude that either encourages or allows us to lie, then we will lie when the opportunity arises. We need to set a personal expectation in our minds, ahead of time, that it is not acceptable to lie.

Through Advanced Thought Planning you need to decide ahead of time that you are not a liar! This is your Big Decision. (See the Introduction for a full explanation of these two concepts). This decision must be made 'once and for all,' and not mentally debated over and over again as each occasion for lying presents itself during your daily life. I will discuss more on this concept of the Big Decision a little bit later.

As we consider the necessity of being honest, please keep in mind that when speaking the truth, compassion is of great value. That insight is the result of Enlightened Thinking. Let's not unnecessarily hurt anyone's feelings. We can communicate the truth without adopting a brutally honest style. Through Advanced Thought Planning we can learn to express truth and compassion. It's critical that you demonstrate sensitivity to the feelings of others, while simultaneously saying what is necessary in every situation.

Early in my career one of my peers was a strong willed young manager (like me). He and I would often have very brutal, honest conversations that only ended because our mutual boss would intervene after a painful hour or two. On one occasion our boss did not intervene, and that conversation nearly came to physical blows. We stopped ourselves; we learned to control ourselves out of respect for one another.

From that day forward I learned that I am responsible for communicating honestly and with respect for my teammates. My self-talk changed to reinforce mature behavior. My Stinking Thinking that had caused me to belittle my teammate stopped and my behavior changed for the better. Our project went on to become enormously successful.

EXAGGERATION

One of the most common forms of lying is exaggeration. There is a great temptation in business to exaggerate and to take credit for things that you did not really accomplish. It's all about making me look good, especially to the boss. It's sometimes called 'managing up,' but it is a subtle form of lying.

This behavior is particularly damaging to teamwork. Fellow team members will retaliate in kind if they feel that someone else is trying to take credit for results that are due to their efforts. Managing up makes everyone on the team suspicious and puts them on alert. Of course, good teamwork is just the opposite. Real teamwork results when everyone is working for the good of the company and not taking the credit for someone else's work.

Think about it: if every person is doing what is best for the company, that's also what is best for each person. We will succeed as a team! And, as a manager we must set the right example. Remember, people are watching you. Your team will do as you do. If you are exaggerating to your boss or teammates, they will eventually realize what you are doing to make yourself look good. This habit can't be sustained over time, because you must exaggerate more and more to maintain the illusion of progress. Eventually the real, limited accomplishments are known to all.

In today's financial world, we have all become familiar with 'Ponzi' schemes. In these schemes the financial manager constantly promises bigger financial returns to his clients, but in reality he is secretively breaking even or losing money. He tries to cover over his loses with new investments from new clients. These schemes are unsustainable, and can't last for more than a period of a few months or at the most, a few years. Often at the bitter end, the manager who exaggerates is fired, and may even go to jail for breaking the law.

In our self-talk I believe that we excuse exaggeration through Stinking Thinking. We think that it doesn't really hurt anyone, and of course we think that "everyone does it." Well if we do some Advanced Thought Planning about this, we have to agree that it does hurt someone. The person who is hurt is the one that is denied the rightful credit for their accomplishment.

If we really think about it, the excuse that "everyone does it" is not an excuse for any behavior. This is just a rationalization that occurs in our minds at the instant of our lying behavior. If we spend quality time in Advanced Thought Planning, seriously contemplating the ethical aspects of exaggeration, we must conclude that it is wrong. Furthermore, we will also conclude that it destroys teamwork. People will know that we are exaggerating and they will simply not like it. The moral of this story is that we need to think about this behavior ahead of time. We need to make the Big Decision: tell the honest facts all of the time.

LYING

Then of course there is the possibility of blatantly lying, when it feels necessary. As you read this, you are probably thinking (another example of self-talk) that few professional people would do this. Oh really? Do people lie on their tax returns, or on company expense accounts, or in calculating corporate revenue, or in back dating stock options?

Unfortunately many, many people do exactly that, as we all know from news reports of corporate corruption. This trend is getting worse. *Forbes* magazine recently documented that 90 percent of high school students admitted to cheating on tests. That's about triple the rate found in a survey conducted in 1963.[3] These high school students will eventually become employees in the workforce, and many will become managers. Will these people be trustworthy? Unfortunately, I think not unless they change their thinking and their behavior.

And, yes, in my career I've had many occasions of managers outright lying to me. In one notable example I had signed a software cooperation contract with a partner company while I was employed at HP. Later that CEO failed to deliver anything specified in the contract. When we confronted him with the delinquency, he simply suggested that if we didn't like it we could sue him. Well, it wasn't worth the time or the cost of a lawsuit. So we cancelled the contract and moved on with other business. That particular CEO was later fired for other illegal activities at his company. In addition he had also falsified his college degrees.

People who lie usually build a habit that they can't easily stop. This form of Stinking Thinking is habit forming. It's like a bank robber who has robbed his first bank and escaped successfully. He soon is tempted to rob another bank; his self-talk convinces him that he won't be caught. This bank robbing behavior continues until he is eventually arrested. Bad habits are very difficult to break! Only through Advanced Thought Planning can we analyze these habits and make the Big Decision to change.

I learned that even professionals lie. Maybe I was naive to think that professional people would have exceptional integrity. I have also learned that it's impossible to work with people who lie. When dealing with someone who I knew had a past history of lying, I never could be sure if I was hearing the truth. If you have someone like that on your team, you can never be sure what has really been accomplished or completed on a given task. Maybe they are exaggerating their results, or maybe the task is done but with poor quality. After all, quality means attention to details, and just maybe the task was not really done properly; and now the person is misleading you.

You don't want to have to manage a project while being suspicious about someone. And you certainly don't want to put your boss in that situation.

Don't ever be so driven for success that you compromise your integrity.

It's not worth it! In fact, it will not work over the long term anyway. If you lie, you will be discovered. We are back to the same Big Decision: tell the honest facts all of the time.

Focus your mind on Enlightened Thinking and minimize Stinking Thinking. Only through this conscious self-talk can you change your behavior.

TEAMMATES

My advice is: say what you mean and mean what you say. Secondly, my advice is: hire people with this style of integrity. In a recent management survey, *InformationWeek* magazine reported that ethics and morals have become the number one hiring criteria in the computer industry.[4] Unfortunately it's becoming very common for people to exaggerate, lie, and fail to live up to their commitments.

If you commit to be somewhere, or do something, or deliver something; just do it. People are counting on you, and of course you are counting on other people. Consider these wise words by Senior Pastor Dave Sawkins in San Jose, California: "The greatest ability is dependability." Think about it. If people at work or at home can't count on your word, then managing well and gaining success is probably impossible.

Behavioral economics researcher Dan Ariely conducted an interesting experiment in human psychology related to integrity.[5] In this particular experiment college students were presented with an opportunity to cheat on a test. Most of them did cheat, not realizing that the psychology researchers could identify their cheating. This experiment was repeated many times at several colleges with the same result.

However, one group of students were asked to write down as many of the Ten Commandments as they could recall before taking the test. Immediately they were given the same opportunity to cheat as the other student groups. Amazingly none of the students in this special group cheated on their test. When this experiment was repeated, the results were the same. The students who were asked to recall the

Ten Commandments beforehand didn't cheat. Why did the students' behavior change? How did the students' thinking get modified?

The researchers concluded that in order to raise the level of integrity in our society, it would serve us well to simply remind ourselves of the importance of integrity! Think about it: the simple recollection of the Ten Commandments triggers Enlightened Thinking. And of course, proper behavior is the result of Enlightened Thinking.

Furthermore, I believe that by actually teaching the importance of integrity, we can stimulate students to do the proper Advanced Thought Planning. If students are encouraged to do this thinking, they will most likely make the appropriate Big Decision: be honest. In the very early years of the Ivy League colleges, integrity was routinely taught by professors as an inherent part of many courses.

It will positively serve our society if we encourage our citizens to speak the truth, always. This thought process and resulting behavior is not just a lifestyle choice, but rather it is an imperative to a stable society.

PERSONAL APPLICATION

1) How many times did you exaggerate with someone today?
2) Do you have a regular habit of lying?
3) Why?
4) Write down your Big Decision:

<u>INTEGRITY</u>

SAY WHAT YOU MEAN

MEAN WHAT YOU SAY

AND, JUST DO IT

****

REMEMBER PEOPLE ARE WATCHING
YOU

****

THE GREATEST ABILITY IS
DEPENDABILITY

SELF-TALK on INTEGRITY

ADVANCED THOUGHT PLANNING:

WHO WILL I HURT BY LYING?

WHY AM I INCLINED TO EXAGGERATE?

WHAT WILL I LOSE IF I COMPROMISE MY INTEGRITY?

****

THE BIG DECISION:

I WILL SPEAK THE TRUTH AT ALL TIMES

Chapter Two

Humility – Focus on Others

———— ❦ ————

KEY POINT:
Humble people do not dwell on themselves. They think about how to help others first.

STINKING THINKING:
It's all about me; how can I win?

ENLIGHTENED THINKING:
I am a person of strength who gives a great deal to people around me. We will succeed as a team!

Your style is how people perceive you. Let's do a little Advanced Thought Planning on how you would like people to perceive you. It's not mandatory, but as a manager it's extremely advantageous for people to like you and to know that they can rely upon you. Being friendly and cordial, with humility, really doesn't take that much energy and it will give you the benefit of the doubt with your team. After all, haven't you really appreciated bosses with whom you liked to be with at work? But it's even more important that people know that they can trust you.

It's ironic that Richard Nixon, in a campaign commercial for Barry Goldwater in 1964, said the following: "With all the power that a President has, the most important thing to bear in mind is this: you must not give power to a man unless, above everything else, he has character. Character is the most important qualification the President of the United States can have." Years later Richard Nixon went on to fail miserably as a President because of his poor character. Managers in most companies also wield a large amount of power. If you have power without character be very careful. Think about it.

With that imperative let's consider our next character trait. Let's take a look at the character trait of humility. This topic is one of my favorites because I struggle with it the most. In our American society we are always told that 'it's all about me.' In fact, a huge shopping mall here in Silicon Valley has an oversized billboard with the mall's name and the slogan: "It's All About You."

However, it is interesting that most of us prefer to work with humble people rather than with arrogant people. A humble person is a person who just doesn't dwell on themself. Humility does not imply that the person is boring or simple.

People who are humble practice Enlightened Thinking. They are more concerned with how you and how the team is doing, rather than themselves. Humble people are easy to work with because they focus on team success, and we tend to like them for that attitude. Their humility builds us up as they compliment and encourage us. They actually trigger Enlightened Thinking in us!

So each of us should strive to be humble! Doesn't that make sense? Unfortunately most of us are not humble. I think it's because, in our Stinking Thinking, we are afraid that other people who are not humble will take advantage of us in some way. In our defensiveness we focus on ourselves, which of course then triggers Stinking Thinking in the people around us. All of this fearful thinking results from an improper definition of humility.

Many people think that being humble means to demean themselves, or to not represent themselves well. Or, even worse, some people think that humility means that they should walk around with their head hanging down, letting other people take advantage of them.

Real humility is simply being yourself; no more and no less.

That means that we admit to our limitations, and that we are confident of our capabilities. We should desire to work cooperatively with our teammates. If someone does try to take advantage of us, we can politely discuss the issue with that person.

It's important that we know ourselves very well.

We need to have a correct self-image; we need to practice a lot of Advanced Thought Planning. Make a list of the things in which you are competent, and list the things in which you could improve. Ask people around you to help you complete the list. (By the way if you don't want to ask others to help you with your list, you're probably not humble.)

Also, it might be useful to do one list at your workplace, and another with your family at home. I'm sure that your spouse will want to help you with your list of needed improvements. As you build your lists of strengths and opportunities for improvements, please seriously consider which attributes you actually know to be true about yourself. You may find some of your strengths hard to really believe. Or, you may reject some of the areas for improvement that were suggested by friends. Sometimes the people close to us can see our personalities better than we can ourselves. Your self-talk on these topics may be the result of decades of Stinking Thinking. But through Advanced Thought Planning you can make the appropriate Big Decisions about who you really are and who you want to be in the future. My experience is that very few people actually know themselves accurately.

For example many times in my career I have had people tell me that I'm an excellent speaker. But every time I see myself giving a speech on a video, I don't like what I see and hear. Earlier in my career this Stinking Thinking often caused me to avoid public forums. It has taken many decades for me to replace the Stinking Thinking with this Enlightened Thinking: I am a very good speaker. And, through a lot of Advanced Thought Planning I have reached a Big Decision: I enjoy speaking and I'm a very good speaker. As a result of this self-talk, my behavior has changed. I no longer avoid public forums.

TEAMMATES

If you practice humility, your team will very quickly follow in your footsteps.

Enlightened Thinking is contagious!

Your team will become more cohesive and supportive of one another. I saw this happen at Xilinx. Bernie Vonderschmitt, who was the founder of the company, quickly built a $1 billion company as a humble, customer —and employee— focused executive. He cared a great deal about other people. As a result of Bernie's role model, Xilinx was always rated number one in customer service compared to our competitors.

In another example Bill Hewlett and Dave Packard did the same thing as founders of HP, and their legacy continues decades later. HP's customers and business partners still have a strong appreciation for the company's customer focused culture.

The opposite of course is very evident all around the world. CEOs who are arrogant and quick tempered can destroy teamwork and the whole company. These CEOs often come to believe that they know more than they really do, and they often begin to think that they are above the law as well. Eventually reality does catch up with them, and unfortunately many people suffer. And, it gets even worse. Employees of companies will often take on the persona of their CEO to the detriment of the overall business. Stinking Thinking is also contagious! We can all name companies that started out strong, but under the influence of a poor

CEO, became internally focused and eventually failed. Great leaders will keep the focus of work on the customer and not on themselves.

The bottom line is: humble managers are appreciated by their teammates, stockholders, and by their customers as well.

What do you think? What is your self-talk 'saying?'

PERSONAL APPLICATION

1) Is your self-image accurate or prideful?
2) Have you made a list of your strengths and opportunities for improvement?
3) Is it all about me, or the team?
4) Write down your Big Decision:

HUMILITY

**BE HUMBLE – FOCUS ON THE SUCCESS
OF YOUR TEAM**

****

**HUMILITY TRIGGERS ENLIGHTENED
THINKING IN YOUR TEAM**

****

**MY TEAM, AND I TOGETHER,
WILL SUCCEED**

SELF-TALK on HUMILITY

ADVANCED THOUGHT PLANNING:
DO I KNOW WHO I REALLY AM?
DO I APPRECIATE MYSELF?
DO I WANT TO HELP OTHERS?

****

THE BIG DECISION:
I WILL BE HUMBLE

Chapter Three

Joyfulness – Enjoy Life

———⟨∞⟩———

KEY POINT:
People tend to think clearly and creatively when they are relaxed.

STINKING THINKING:
I feel lousy and I don't care who notices my mood. Besides, these people are a pain in the neck.

ENLIGHTENED THINKING:
Today will be productive if I lighten up and positively focus on success.

Let's move on to discuss joyfulness. I'm not necessarily talking about someone who has lost touch with reality and is always trying to be happy despite the circumstances. Nor am I suggesting that you should try to become a comedian. Stand-up comedy is not easy!

I am suggesting that, most of the time, you should try to maintain a positive, lighthearted attitude at work. This Enlightened Thinking will allow you and your teammates to think more clearly and creatively, raising the likelihood of success. When we become too negatively emotional, our minds often become clouded with swirling confused thoughts. We may not be able to separate key issues like our self-worth from the status of a project that we are responsible for managing.

There is a clear business payoff to joyfulness.

Several recent studies documented in *SmartMoney* magazine indicate that people's productivity improved by 12 percent when their mood was positive.[6] In addition, people who were optimistic were more likely to be promoted within two years of starting a new job. And, *Fortune* magazine's "100 Best Companies to Work For" financially outperformed similar companies on the stock market.[7] You will be more successful when you are joyful!

With that motivation, let's do some Advanced Thought Planning about joyfulness. When have you discovered your best ideas? When have you been able to perform at your best? I doubt that your best thinking occurred when someone was intimidating you at a business meeting! When we are intimidated our thoughts tend to get focused on defending ourselves. And, the same is true of people around you.

So it's best if other people feel at ease while you are present; as a result they will be more likely to be effective in your presence. Remember: if you are someone's manger (or manager's manager), there is already a significant amount of unintentional intimidation occurring in your presence for many employees. If everyone is relaxed, they will be able to think more clearly, and creatively as well. They will be focused on the business at hand, rather than thinking about self-protection.

On the other hand if you are always serious, demanding, or intense, that behavior will actually drain energy from the people around you. They will feel the need to keep their guard up to protect themselves from your tough attitude. You will have triggered their Stinking Thinking.

They will be thinking about methods to protect themselves from you.

As a leader wouldn't you prefer that the people you are leading are thinking about creative ways to resolve the issues being discussed? If you trigger a defensive mindset, it causes energy to be wasted that instead could be used more productively. You have a significant impact on the self-talk of people, and upon their productivity!

Let's do some intense Advanced Thought Planning about your attitude at work. What Stinking Thinking has led you to be less than friendly with people? Are you afraid of failure? Are you afraid that if people get to know the 'real' you, they may reject you? Is your self-talk centered on your perception of what other people might be thinking about you? Do you think of yourself in a negative manner? Does that self-talk lead you to think that other people perceive you negatively?

Now that you are doing Advanced Thought Planning can you 'hear' the voices that are circling viciously in your mind? The circular thought is: if I don't really like myself then I'm inclined to think that other people don't like me either. The Stinking Thinking goes on: if someone doesn't like me then why should I like them. This is an unfortunate perfect example of Stinking Thinking. Based upon my experience, this is very common to the human species. It's also quite common to become very angry in the midst of this Stinking Thinking. It's easy for our emotions to get out of control when we think someone doesn't like us. So, what is the solution? How can Advanced Thought Planning lead to a Big Decision, and much better human interaction?

The key Big Decision is: I have many reasons to be joyful.

This decision starts with accepting myself as a valuable person. If I am valuable, then there are many good reasons to be joyful. The future always looks better when I have confidence in myself. My present attitude is always best when the future looks positive. Also, this Big Decision includes accepting others as valuable people as well. Otherwise, as humans we are prone to think of ourselves too highly.

If we find ourselves thinking that we're more important than others, then that attitude causes us to get defensive when we think someone is about to attack us. That Stinking Thinking may also trigger us to put other people down, needlessly becoming critical and judgmental. We need to maintain positive self-talk about ourselves and about other people. That Enlightened Thinking will enable us to be joyful and encouraging. In addition, with a positive self-image we can even politely respond to a perceived attack from a teammate.

I've been in many meetings when a peer had seemingly disparaged my suggestions for a new product. In that situation it's far too easy to get emotional and respond in an equally disparaging manner. In the midst of Stinking Thinking you may jump to the conclusion that the critic intends to harm you. If you are prepared with a positive self-image, isn't it best to simply ask for a further explanation of the perceived attack? Instead of triggering a confrontation you may learn important facts through this person's criticism. In fact I usually found that there was no intended attack at all. Sometimes by remaining calm, I learned about a very strong suggestion for an improvement to the product. However, there were a few times when I was being attacked! My calm response thwarted the attack in a professional manner. In either situation it is best to be positive and joyful in our self-talk, leading to a calm demeanor and positive behavior.

TEAMMATES

How can we best use this Enlightened Thinking to help set a joyful tone in an organization? First, make sure that your demeanor is positive and encouraging. And, make sure to tell your face to smile so that other people can see your positive feelings. Be sure to express your feelings verbally. It's always helpful to congratulate people for their successes. We need to take time and dwell on the things that are going well, even when there are problems. (There are always at least a few problems.) If you happen to be in a nasty mood, maybe it would be better to avoid human interaction. Spend the time in your office.

Second, let employees know that you have a sense of humor. When I was in a meeting with many organizational levels present, periodically when the opportunity arose, I would politely poke fun at myself. I would talk about something that I had done that was not 'too smart.' It's useful for employees to know that you have a sense of humor.

Third, at the beginning of the meeting while everyone is getting settled in, you can simply talk about a funny event that occurred while you were on vacation. Or, just ask others how their day is going. Ask them about their kids, their spouse, or their car. Show that you care about the people around you. One senior manager on our team was far too intense most of the time. I learned that I could get him to lighten-up at work by asking him about his car. He just loved to talk about his BMW. This light conversation helped everyone get relaxed before the meeting began.

Of course, there is a time to be serious. If you are dealing with important issues or problems, it's best to be serious. However, make sure that people perceive you as someone who is balanced and who enjoys life. Yes, let's be sure to enjoy life!

You and I have a choice. Will we remain calm and joyful in the midst of our endeavors? Or, will we make life more difficult for ourselves and those around us? (For more thoughts on this topic please read: "What Really Matters in Life" in the Appendix.)

PERSONAL APPLICATION

1) How do people perceive your moods?
2) Do you remind yourself of your successes, and to be positive?
3) Do you need to encourage your teammates more often?
4) Write down your Big Decision:

JOYFULNESS

ENJOY LIFE

****

**YOU AND YOUR TEAM
WILL BE MORE PRODUCTIVE**

SELF-TALK on JOYFULNESS

ADVANCED THOUGHT PLANNING:

AM I SETTING THE RIGHT TEAM ENVIRONMENT?

AM I ENJOYING MY WORK?

****

THE BIG DECISION:

I AM A VALUABLE PERSON

AND

I HAVE MANY REASONS TO BE JOYFUL

Chapter Four

Openness – You Can't Hide

—⁂—

KEY POINT:
I will let people get to know the real me. I will be open with my teammates.

STINKING THINKING:
My faults are best kept hidden. No one will like me if they really know me.

ENLIGHTENED THINKING:
People can see my strengths and weaknesses every day. My team accepts me for who I am. I am a valuable human being.

L et's move on to discuss openness. As children we often learn to hide our bad behavior. We also often learn to hide the bad results of our projects.

I can still remember as a fourth grader receiving a poor report card. My first thoughts were to keep the report card hidden from my parents. How's that for Stinking Thinking? It didn't work. Back in those days parents and teachers communicated with each other very often. My parents eventually were told about my poor grades. During those several days of hiding my report card, my mind was consumed with fear. My results at school got even worse. Based on this simple childhood example, we can do some Advanced Thought Planning about being open.

The bottom line is: when we try to hide who we are, there are two bad things that will happen. First, usually we will eventually fail to keep ourselves hidden. And, second, our self-talk becomes negative and unproductive; we are mentally distracted from topics that really matter.

The key lesson to be learned is: just be open, and as a result, our self-talk will be positively empowered.

How is that for Enlightened Thinking?

There are even more benefits to openness. If you are perceived as open, people are more likely to be open with you about themselves as well. You can easily instigate an atmosphere of Enlightened Thinking. Your teammates will share with you information about the challenges that they are fighting on the job. You will learn about the real status of their project; the good and the bad results. And most important, you will learn about their concerns for the future of the project so you can take preventative action early, before a failure occurs.

Whatever your attitude is toward being open in your communication with people, I would suggest that you push yourself to communicate even more! Try to set a great example for your team. There is an old saying that people need to hear something seven times before it really connects with them.

To make these situations even worse, we humans have a habit of under-communicating. Our Stinking Thinking could be the result of simple laziness or our mistaken belief that the other person doesn't really have a need to know. In either case, we need to strive to communicate well.

Now, here is one of the most important aspects of openness: if you demonstrate openness, people may share with you their thoughts of what you could do to improve or change yourself.

When your teammates help you improve yourself, you have really struck gold. None of us are perfect. It's always useful to collect input about how we can improve ourselves and our results. Keep in mind that most people will not tell you what they are really thinking about you, but it is worth asking them anyway (read the discussion in Chapter Six concerning Difficult Conversations).

One of the best ways to demonstrate openness is to ask your teammates for feedback about yourself, and then graciously accept the offered feedback. In addition, when people experience your willingness to listen to feedback, they will become open to feedback as well. You must set the proper example. In fact, be sure to be conscious of how you listen to your teammates. Don't be rehearsing your response to criticism while you are trying to listen. People can tell if you are listening to their thoughts or not. Really pay attention to what people are trying to tell you.

Many years ago at a management conference we had a session on Enlightened Thinking, and I learned about the 'blue chip.' The idea was to identify one thing about myself that, if I improved, would make a large difference in my results on the job. This personal item could be a weakness to be improved, but it was most often one of my strengths, that I could further strengthen. Usually our strengths will out-weigh our weaknesses in terms of leveraging personal success. That one item became my 'blue chip' or my most valuable item to work on for personal improvement. (In a gambling casino the blue poker chip is the most valuable chip in the establishment.) This planning activity became a perfect example of Advanced Thought Planning in regards to openness.

In order to ingrain this resulting Enlightened Thinking in my mind, I would carry a blue poker chip in my pocket for 60 days to remind myself of the personal item I was striving to improve during this period in time. I would also ask other people to help me with my 'blue chip' item. People came to feel at ease with this process, and they would routinely ask me what my 'blue chip' was at that time. I could ask them the same question.

There was a lot of Enlightened Thinking around the topic of 'blue chips.' It became very exciting to be able to have friendly discussions aimed at self-improvement for myself, as well as for others. This technique really initiated helpful conversations between managers and their staffs. A great deal of the normal defensiveness that occurs during employee performance appraisals just seemed to disappear.

Everyone realized that appraisals were designed to help us all improve the company's results through our own self-improvement. Advanced Thought Planning on the topic of self-improvement became an institutionalized process.

Finally, on the topic of openness, here is a very daring challenge: let's be open with our bosses. Let's ask our managers for their thoughts on how we can improve our contribution to the company. Let's not let our self-talk get dominated by fear. Remember that improving one of your strengths will often be the subject of this conversation. Ask your boss for feedback and then quietly listen; don't argue with the feedback. Turn off any Stinking Thinking triggered by this conversation. Write down your manager's thoughts and then go home and think about what you heard. The next time you meet with your manager in private you can ask questions, and if necessary, have some debate. If your boss won't tell you what he is thinking because you're not open to the feedback, your boss will still be thinking those thoughts about you anyway!

It really is best to know what your boss is thinking about you even if you don't like what you may hear.

With your manager's input you can now do a bit of Advanced Thought Planning. You can begin to analyze this input and possibly put a 'blue chip' in place that positively responds to your boss's input. This process is sure to trigger some Enlightened Thinking about you, in the mind of your manager!

PERSONAL APPLICATION

1) Is there anything you tried to hide today?
2) Do teammates know that you want and value their feedback?

3) Do you know what your boss thinks about you?
4) Write down your Big Decision:

OPENNESS

PEOPLE SEE MY STRENGTHS AND WEAKNESSES

✳✳✳✳

WHAT'S YOUR BLUE CHIP?

I'LL TELL YOU IF YOU TELL ME

SELF-TALK on OPENNESS

ADVANCED THOUGHT PLANNING:

HIDING THE TRUTH WILL FAIL

HOW CAN I ASK PEOPLE TO HELP ME?

HOW CAN I ASK MY BOSS FOR INPUT?

****

THE BIG DECISION:

JUST BE OPEN

Chapter Five

Trust – Be Faithful

———∞∞∞———

KEY POINT:
Conducting business requires a high degree of trust.
I must model trustworthiness.

STINKING THINKING:
I can't trust anyone. I'll just keep my eyes open and
be on my guard.

ENLIGHTENED THINKING:
I am trustworthy and I expect the same of my work
associates.

Let's move on to discuss trust. This character trait is crucial to the operation of a business and to a democratic government. Free trade requires that people in business trust one another.

For example if I purchase a home through a bank mortgage, the bank is trusting that I will make the payments as promised by my signature. And, I am trusting that the bank will provide the purchase funds as specified in the mortgage. If either party in this transaction lies and fails to fulfill their commitments, then there will be no profit for either party. With the decline in the housing market during the past few years, this simple transaction has become perverted. Stinking Thinking dominates the financial industry.

There is now a severe lack of trust, which has significantly delayed the recovery of the housing market and our entire economy. Many homeowners whose home values have dramatically declined no longer want to make their mortgage payments (their value is 'under water'). In addition, some banks are now attempting to execute foreclosures without proper documentation. In many of these cases, it is not clear who really legally owns the home! In this housing market, where there is a lack of trust, it has become very difficult to buy or sell a home. As a result, the housing market continues to suffer, impacting the overall economic recovery.

Our government can only be effective if trust is present between the leaders and the citizens. In a recent *Forbes* magazine article entitled: "Wanted: Someone to Trust," author Paul Johnson explained his Enlightened Thinking: "The processes of earning and granting trust are gradual and almost metaphysical. So it is that a good leader, at some point, ceases to be merely a politician, an officeholder; he or she becomes a trusted institution. And from that point on the nation becomes healthier, more secure and thus happier." [8]

Let's do some serious Advanced Thought Planning about trust and team dynamics. Trust in the workplace is also a two-way street. First, we managers should trust people in general.

We may work with many people whom we don't really know very well, and, we need to be able to initially trust them!

We need to give people the benefit of the doubt, unless, there is concrete evidence that they are not trustworthy. For our own mental health, it's best to be a trusting person. Suspicion can drain a lot of your mental energy, and teammates don't like it at all when they are under suspicion. Through this Advanced Thought Planning we can make the Big Decision that even though everyone may not be trustworthy, we are still better off if we trust our teammates. Then when an occasion arises that appears to be questionable, you will quickly react in a trusting manner. This trusting reaction will help to encourage team work. It is also usually true, that people will behave in the manner that we expect of them. Enlightened Thinking is contagious.

In my experience if someone doesn't deserve your trust, concrete evidence will become available surprisingly quickly.

At that point, with concrete evidence, my advice is to confront that person in a professional way. It is very difficult to work with someone whom you don't trust. It's actually better for one of you to find another job. I know that this is not always practical. In such cases you will have to keep your eyes open and be on guard, but it's still best to discuss these trust issues with the other person as they arise. And unfortunately, these bad behaviors do tend to be repetitive. But there is always hope that your teammate will change their behavior, especially if there is an overall culture of honesty within the team.

If you are this person's manager, I suggest that you seriously consider asking them to either change their behavior or leave the company. In some cases it may even be necessary to collect evidence for a dismissal case. But, it is most important that you don't fall victim to the Stinking Thinking that if one person is not trustworthy then no one deserves your trust. I believe that it is better to be trusting even if, periodically, someone takes advantage of you. You just don't want to live your life absorbed by suspicion.

The second key aspect of trust is that we should be trustworthy ourselves.

People in our lives should know that they can trust us.

Think about it! I am amazed at the number of high profile people who wind up in a divorce after they have cheated on their spouse. These people then expect to be effective and trusted in their careers. Unfortunately, I believe that the same Stinking Thinking that has led to infidelity in marriage will also have an impact on their careers. Personally I believe that if someone has habitually lied to their spouse, then they will most likely lie to their friends and work associates as well. If you follow the guidelines in Chapter One concerning integrity, then trustworthiness is the result in all of your relationships. Integrity is simply being honest with everybody, including your spouse and your work associates.

If you are honest with people, they will eventually trust you. You have earned their trust. The best Enlightened Thinking in this situation is to realize that I am setting the role model for how people around me will behave. If I am trustworthy, then the people who surround me will most likely be trustworthy as well. In my experience, most people want to live-up to the high expectations of a strong leader. People do not want to disappoint the person whom they respect.

DELIVERING BAD NEWS

One critical aspect of trust that is often overlooked is to honestly deliver bad news. I think that we have all suffered through difficult projects at work. Let's take the case of a project that is running behind schedule. It happens quite frequently. Do we accurately report the status of the schedule at the monthly review meetings? Management is trusting that we do exactly that, on a regular basis. But, of course, the management will be less than happy when they hear the bad news. So, it's very tempting in the midst of Stinking Thinking to make our report sound better than the actual reality.

The Stinking Thinking in this circumstance is very powerful. For apparent self-protection I may think: why should I deliver the bad news? Or I may think: we can fix this next month before anyone finds out the truth. I believe that we can only resist this temptation to lie through strong Advanced Thought Planning!

Please think about it and make the Big Decision that you will be trustworthy, even in difficult situations.

As a manager I always encouraged everyone to be open and honest. I definitely wanted to be able to trust that I was receiving accurate reports. If we really understand the status of a project, then it's possible to discuss the issues and take the appropriate actions quickly. In fact the sooner that we take corrective action the better the outcome will be. As a team we need to trust in each other's reporting of the facts. As a manager it's always best to report the blunt facts both to your group and to your boss. Be sure to set the proper example at all times.

TRUSTING MY OPINION

Enlightened Thinking about trust also includes being open and honest about what you don't know. If you want people to trust you, and you want your team to be successful, don't try to fool them into thinking that you are knowledge-able in a certain arena. You can sadly mislead someone to a false conclusion, with poor results for your entire team. For example if I am naive about some technical arena that is important to my job, I should be open about that reality. Yes, tell your boss and co-workers that that's the way it is. Then it will be possible for your team to compensate for your short-coming, and raise the chances for your team's success.

If you hide your naiveté, it could lead to failure for everyone.

It's fairly common in meetings for everyone to act like they 'know it all.' I've been shocked to discover that many people in meetings did not understand some topic under dis-cussion until finally one person had the courage to ask for an explanation and admit their ignorance. Many other people in that meeting may have had the same lack of understanding, but they chose to fake their knowledge to avoid admitting the truth. They were trying to make themselves 'look good.' It's best to go ahead and ask a question that may sound dumb. If you are willing to admit what you don't know, then people can trust you about what you claim to actually know. I'll discuss this topic further in Chapter Six in the section "Know What You Don't Know."

PERSONAL APPLICATION

1) Are you behaving in a manner that is completely trustworthy?
2) Do you trust everyone on your team?
3) Do you need to professionally confront someone about their lack of trustworthiness?
4) Write down your Big Decision:

TRUST

WHEN IN DOUBT, BE TRUSTING

✳✳✳✳

CONFRONT WITH EVIDENCE ANYONE YOU SUSPECT OF LYING

✳✳✳✳

BE TRUSTWORTHY, ESPECIALLY, IN TOUGH SITUATIONS

✳✳✳✳

ADMIT TO WHAT YOU DON'T KNOW

SELF-TALK on TRUST

ADVANCED THOUGHT PLANNING:

WAS I TRUSTWORTHY TODAY?

DO I TRUST PEOPLE I DON'T KNOW?

HOW CAN I BE A TRUSTING PERSON EVEN IF SOMEONE HAS FAILED ME?

****

THE BIG DECISION:

I WILL TRUST MY TEAM

I AM TRUSTWORTHY AT ALL TIMES

Chapter Six

Be Aggressive –
Take Smart Risks

KEY POINT:
Be intelligently aggressive in everything you do; remember that without risk there is usually little to gain.

STINKING THINKING:
I can't succeed so why bother trying and failing. I will look bad! After all, I am just an average person.

ENLIGHTENED THINKING:
I can excel today and deliver my best results. I will learn from my mistakes. I will succeed!

Taking smart risks is the first and probably the most important leadership principle; and, it's also one of the most difficult principles to master. It's very common for a manager to be either too aggressive, and take too much risk in setting goals, or to be not aggressive enough and take too little risk. It requires a great deal of solid thinking to find the proper balance in your decisions.

A manager who is aggressive must also be steadfast; you can't be too quick to change directions. Sometimes an aggressive person can abandon an idea too quickly in favor of a newer idea. But on the other hand, a wise manager must know when it is time to stop and change direction. We must learn from our mistakes. Steadfastness is a virtue, but stubbornness can lead to a disaster. These leadership challenges can sound like a contradiction, but I'd rather call them a paradox.

In this chapter, I will explore these challenges of proper balance in regards to aggressive thinking. We will attempt to do some Advanced Thought Planning on the topic of risk taking and being an aggressive leader. (I have had several people tell me that they do not like my use of the word 'aggressive.' The connotation can imply that there is some personally offensive aspect to the actions of an *aggressive* person. Possibly a better choice for my purposes would be to utilize the word 'assertive.' However, while I do not condone any personally offensive action on anyone's part, I prefer the assertive connotation of the word 'aggressive.' Hopefully you will accept or at least tolerate my choice of terminology.)

As you contemplate a business decision, be very aware of your self-talk.

You need to consider if you are naturally too aggressive, or possibly too risk adverse.

Each of us has an inner voice that can emotionally impact our thinking and decisions. The challenge is to balance your enthusiasm with your risk aversion. You need to calibrate yourself on this balance. What is your self-talk around the topic of making decisions and managing risk? Some people, in my experience, get carried away with their enthusiasm. They may fall in love with their own new idea or invention, and miss the harsh reality of the business situation. They will pursue their idea to the ends-of-the-earth, to their own detriment. Yes, it's important to be tough and steadfast as we face challenges, but don't become blind to likely future failure. Do not let your aggressive self-talk deceive you into being overly optimistic about the future. Be sure to do some Advanced Thought Planning that includes establishing clear milestones for your endeavor. These milestones should be measurable and unavoidable (see Chapter Nine: "Measure It – Or Don't Do It").

I believe that most people are actually risk-adverse and lack enough enthusiasm for risk-taking. I can still remember that as a young engineer at Bell Labs I was completely intimidated when I saw my director walking towards me in the hallway. I quickly decided to say nothing and try to smile. Unfortunately, most of our self-talk is to fear failure and we dwell extensively in Stinking Thinking. Our self-talk can be dominated by worries of failure. We consequently often procrastinate and don't even get started with the pursuit of our dream. Or, after starting an endeavor, we throttle back our aggressiveness because we become overwhelmed with the fear of failure. We don't really get fully committed to our own success.

Here's a simple example that often occurs on the job. Imagine that your boss drops into your cubicle and mentions that there is a meeting next week with several people and your company's top VP. Your boss explains that you are scheduled to give a presentation at that meeting. How do you react? What is your self-talk? You may confidently think that this meeting is a great opportunity for you to express your ideas to the top VP. You may quickly start planning to give the best presentation possible. However, I think most people react by becoming very anxious. Thoughts of failure begin to dominate your thinking. And if you don't get that Stinking Thinking under control, you can't put together an effective presentation for the meeting. To complicate the situation even more, in the midst of self-talk dominated by fear and anxiety, it is extremely difficult to become creative in our thinking.

When fear occupies our minds, we tend to get trapped into tight thought patterns that dwell on one negative subject. Fear defeats creativity!

And in today's business world, creativity is one of the most sought after abilities. CEOs in a recent survey said that they value creativity in their employees above all other abilities.[9] Creativity is required to deal with the myriad of obstacles that we will face in life.

We must plan for success through Enlightened Thinking. We should envision exactly what success will look like in detail. In all situations consciously manage your self-talk to arrive at rational, wise decisions. There must be a balance between wild enthusiasm and fear, but I'd suggest that you error on the side of being more enthusiastic. Leaders actually set the pace for their organization. Go ahead and be aggressive, but with wisdom!

Through Advanced Thought Planning, I believe that it is also necessary to proactively manage what material we will read and think about during the course of our day. What inputs do we allow into our thought processes? If we constantly contemplate negative topics then our self-talk will become negatively dominated. On the other hand if we only contemplate positive topics we will become too optimistic. As an example let's consider our favorite football team. If we constantly read articles that articulate all of the reasons why they will become the next Super Bowl champions, then we are likely to think that there is a high probability of their success. However, we need to manage our reading so that our thinking is rationally balanced to reality, including input on some negative realities.

We need to purposefully construct a plan that provides realistically balanced input to our self-talk on key topics of importance.

(The topic of football may or may not be such a key topic, unless your business is a football franchise.)

Now let's consider several more, key, leadership topics with respect to aggressiveness.

BE AT THE RIGHT PLACE

The most important thing to contemplate, in regards to being aggressive, is to be at the right place at the right time. And, if you determine that you are not at that place, change course sooner rather than later! That is what being aggressive is all about, and it's under your control. You need to think about this and make the Big Decision: do I continue doing what I'm currently doing? For example, let's say that you and your company are working on a new AM/FM radio that will be produced very inexpensively. If it were the 1940's then this new product would have a high probability to become a business success. However, since its 2012, you would be better off to simply forget about the radio. The market for such a product is in the past. (In today's technology a radio is a feature of a smartphone; and it is free.) Either your company needs to change direction, or you need to find a new company. You may be thinking: "Well that's an easy example of an aggressive decision."

The point is rather simple; too many companies pursue products and services that just can't succeed when they are launched into tomorrow's marketplace. Always keep in mind that your product currently under development, must compete not just against current competitors and products, but also against your competitor's future products. The battleground is actually in tomorrow's marketplace. The key competitive issues may be cost, features, or just a lack of customers willing to pay your price. You may be working yourself into exhaustion, but you can fail anyway.

My product rule-of-thumb is that if it is not obviously going to sell extremely well when the product is introduced into the market, then stop what you're doing right now.

You are being aggressive if you stop quickly; or better yet, just don't start such an endeavor. Look for a better option. Only take smart risks. Your self-talk must be realistic, and you must be prepared to take action as the result of Enlightened Thinking.

Similarly, if your current job within your company is at a dead end, and you find that you are becoming disillusioned, it's best to deal with that reality quickly. We humans tend to be fearful of change. But, don't let Stinking Thinking get in your way. Don't be fearful of the future during a period of change. Look for another position within your department that has a brighter future, and request a job reassignment. My experience as a manager is that if you have been doing an excellent job, and you approach your boss for a change, then he/she will do whatever they can to meet your needs quickly. Or, maybe your skills are a better match to a job in another department; if so, request a transfer.

It is always best to aggressively manage your career.

Pursue a job which will allow you to succeed and dream of a better future. I've often wondered why people will often get stuck in their current business activity well after it's become obvious that they are not in the right place at the right time. We often do have a fear of change. But beyond that fear, I believe that we can get paralyzed, because in order to change the situation, we must recognize that we were wrong when earlier we decided to put ourselves into this situation. We actually have to face the reality that we may have made a mistake! Because of the Stinking Thinking involved with our pride, this change can be psychologically very difficult to do in a timely fashion.

The decision to make a change can become very emotionally entangled in our minds. But, one of the keys to success is to quickly learn from our mistakes. This may be one of the biggest challenges that you will face as a leader. Advanced Thought Planning, right now, can lead us to Enlightened Thinking on the topic of change.

We must recognize that everyone makes mistakes, and that successful leaders learn quickly and make the necessary changes.

Another classic example of this prideful Stinking Thinking is in trading common stock on Wall Street. It's psychologically relatively easy to decide to buy a particular stock, but very difficult to decide to sell a stock especially when you are losing money as it declines in value. We are very inclined to hope that the stock price will rebound positively next week. We want to believe that we made a smart decision to buy the stock in the first place. But, before we can emotionally make the proper decision to sell the stock, the stock price may have dropped 25 percent or more. The answer to this debacle is to aggressively deal with our own emotions through Advanced Thought Planning. We must become conscious of our self-talk concerning pride. It's best to predetermine quantified decision triggers. The trigger in this stock market example is possibly a 10 percent loss in the value of the stock calculated from your purchase price.

In a business environment, a possible predetermined trigger to abandon a new product under development could be a 20 percent cost increase, or a six-month delay in the product's schedule. The best way to deal with our emotions is to set these triggers at the beginning of the project. And of course, be sure to document each trigger in detail, so as to avoid rationalizations when the time for a decision has arrived. These triggers must be clear and unavoidable.

EMBRACE DIFFICULT CONVERSATIONS

Another aspect of being an aggressive leader is to have direct and open conversations with everyone. When speaking with fellow workers, be aggressive and get to the point. Certainly don't avoid the point because you are concerned about someone's feelings or even your own feelings. Don't let Stinking Thinking dissuade you from saying what needs to be said clearly. Your self-talk may try to delay the needed conversation. Or you may be less than honest in conveying an embarrassing issue. You need to be tough, and you need to do it with empathy for the people on your team. Get to the point in a professional manner. You can do that without unnecessarily hurting anyone's feelings.

A few years ago I read an excellent book on this subject, *Difficult Conversations* by Douglas Stone.[10] I highly recommend that you read this book together with all of your teammates. In fact at Xilinx we asked every employee to read this book. As a group we were able to do some Advanced Thought Planning and conclude that our team really does prefer direct conversations with each other. We concluded that real issues should be discussed, with the appropriate people.

I believe that many people will often avoid direct conversations because they simply don't want to 'face' the other person. The Stinking Thinking in this situation actually revolves around self-protection. The manager may be insecure and reluctant to lose an argument. Or, the manager may be intimidated by the other person. In any case if you find yourself entangled in this type of self-talk, it's time to stop and think. Ask yourself why you're intimidated? Are you distracted by some Stinking Thinking?

The appropriate Enlightened Thinking will lead you to conclude that avoiding the issue will just prolong the pain for you, and for the other person.

Whenever possible just answer "yes" or "no" to questions, and then explain your thought process. Avoid the Stinking Thinking that says that politicians avoid controversy by being vague, so why shouldn't I do the same thing.

Very often, unfortunately, politicians will avoid giving clear answers when they are interviewed by a reporter. I guess it takes practice to say nothing and yet try to sound intelligent. But, for a real leader, it's best to give clear answers to team member questions. Managing isn't a popularity contest. You will not be popular for very long if your company is a failure because of you.

Another topic closely related to difficult conversations is conducting too many vague meetings. Be aggressive and don't tolerate ineffectiveness. Effective meetings are really difficult conversations planned through Advanced Thought Planning. What is the purpose of the meeting? You must be ready to say "no" to useless meeting proposals. Be aggressive and conduct only a few, short and pointed meetings. Be clear in writing about why you are calling for a meeting, and be clear about what you will discuss at the meeting. People who are invited to the meeting should do their homework, and be well prepared for the stated topics.

If folks are checking their email in your meeting, then you did something wrong either before the meeting or during the meeting. Restructure your meeting plans and make sure that everyone is really engaged in the topic. You may want to reconsider who is invited to the meeting, if all of the attendees are not participating effectively. It would be best to engage in a difficult conversation, and ask them why they are not participating in the meeting.

When the purpose of the meeting is fulfilled, end the meeting. Productivity does matter in successful companies. Be sure to publish the results of your meeting, clearly documenting the decisions and action plans. That way people who were not invited to the meeting for productivity purposes can still be informed about the results of the meeting. Also, be sure to follow up on all of the action items from the meeting. Send out emails to all of the people involved with the topic to document the progress of these action items. Be aggressive and hold people accountable to get these action items completed on time. By the way, if someone invites you to a useless meeting, try to help them either redefine the purpose of the meeting, or, just help them cancel the meeting as soon as is possible.

Another particularly difficult topic of conversation that people prefer to avoid is negotiations. People who are motivated by their Stinking Thinking will often avoid negotiations because they fear that the discussion will become an emotional conflict. Unfortunately, the result of negotiation avoidance is usually measured in paying a high price, in one form or another. This price may be dollar based, a schedule delay, or a strained friendship.

The best way to approach any negotiation is with a plan enabled by Advanced Thought planning. When you plan this difficult conversation, you will minimize your fear and maximize your success. Identify the outcome that you would prefer, and identify how the other person can meet your desired outcome. Also, put yourself in the other person's position. What do you believe is their desired outcome?

Usually it is possible to determine an outcome which allows both of you to be successful.

If the situation truly does not allow mutual success, you should understand your negotiation leverage as early as possible. You should strategically establish a plan that will allow you to succeed. But even in this situation, try to allow for the other person's desired outcome, to the greatest extent possible. In business negotiations, you should aggressively plan for success, but keep in mind that goodwill toward the other person is still the best attitude.

DEMOLISH ROADBLOCKS

The next aspect of being an aggressive manager is to prevent roadblocks from stopping your progress. In fact you should expect roadblocks on a daily basis, and you should expect to resolve them quickly.

As the leader, you will set the speed of the entire organization.

Don't let negative self-talk dominate your thinking and slow down progress in resolving issues. Enlightened Thinking dictates that you have a positive attitude in the midst of resolving the roadblock quickly. When you encounter a roadblock, analyze the situation, resolve the issue, and move on to the next challenge expeditiously. It's usually not necessary to call for extensive meetings and protracted debates.

However, periodically be sure to ask yourself if your current endeavor is still highly likely to be very successful. Ask yourself if it still obvious that you are working on a winning product. It is possible that one of these roadblocks is a big red warning sign about impending failure. After that gut check, if the roadblock is not a red warning sign, push through to the next roadblock, and the next, and so on. Success does require a great deal of determination!

HIRE THE BEST

The next thing about being an aggressive manager is to hire the best person for each job. If you have to pay a little extra to hire the best person, do it. It will be worth the premium over the duration of the project. Many studies have indicated that the best person out performs the average person by more than three times in terms of overall results.

[11] In addition, my experience indicates that the best people will hire the best people.

As a result of hiring the best people, the improvement in overall project results will be multiplied many times over by these 'best' employees.

And of course, I've seen mediocre performers on the job hire other mediocre performers. My suspicion is that the mediocre hiring manager is intimidated by the best candidate. This unfortunate Stinking Thinking will lead us to conclude that the candidate may take our job someday. But if you do hire someone who eventually takes your job, that's real success! An aggressive manager is always looking for their own replacement. Finally when you do hire the best person, be sure to empower them for success. And be sure to take their advice. Yes, ask them for their input on a regular basis.

EXPLOIT TECHNOLOGY

If you are working in a high technology organization, as an aggressive manager be sure to push the critical technologies to your advantage. This is the perfect arena in which to be aggressive. I believe that most of the success in Silicon Valley companies is the result of such aggressiveness.

Technology can be your friend, if, you manage it well.

For a given time period, you can count on certain technologies to improve at a certain rate. For example transistor size in an integrated circuit (Moore's Law) has and will continue to shrink for the next several years. You must plan for that effect, and even exploit it in your product. Similarly cost effective digital communication bandwidth will continue to improve over the next several years.

However, if you and your company are attempting to create a new technology, or a technology improvement discontinuity from the norm, be very careful. It's easy to convince yourself that this discontinuity will happen quickly, but often the time to market reality is much, much longer than most people anticipate.

The current example of this foolish aggressive thinking is with solar power's impact on the generation of electricity; compared to coal, or natural gas. The mainstream media would lead you to believe that solar power can supply most of our nation's electricity now or next year.[12] The reality is that solar power represents only one to two percent of our electrical consumption today. It will likely take decades before solar power can substantially replace electricity produced by coal across our nation.

So yes, be aggressive about technology, but don't be foolish. This is often a very difficult decision to make in any business. Don't let your emotions lead you to Stinking Thinking that is delusional. Advanced Thought Planning is necessary to establish clear measurable milestones. Be sure that you are reading material that is both supportive and critical of the technology that is important to your success. Always be open to both positive and negative input. Don't let yourself get blindsided by new information that you could have had access to, if only you had taken the time to retrieve that information.

KNOW WHAT YOU DON'T KNOW

As an aggressive manager, it is critical that you know what you don't know. We often can innocently delude ourselves into thinking that we are smarter than we really are. This is the ultimate form of Stinking Thinking! I think this is part of the natural human issue of pride. So, actually sit down and force yourself to think about this topic. Do the necessary Advanced Thought Planning to avoid getting blind-sided by your emotions. In fact, sit down with your whole team and document what you do not know. Make a list of the topics that may be important to your success. You may be somewhat shocked to realize how long the list can be.

The Columbia space shuttle disaster is one case to prove this point. The space shuttle had been damaged at liftoff by foam that broke away from the fuel tank. While the shuttle was still in orbit, NASA held meetings to discuss the extent of the damage.[13] One very influential engineering manager in the meetings helped to convince the executives that the foam could probably not have caused significant damage to the shuttle. Unfortunately, he was not an expert in the area of high velocity material ballistics, with these particular materials. He did not know what he didn't know. What was he thinking? As a result of this engineer's opinion (and several other opinions), the shuttle was not inspected in outer space, and it disintegrated during reentry into the earth's atmosphere. Later, ballistic tests proved that it was indeed possible to create very significant damage to the shuttle wing with a high velocity impact of foam.

After you have documented the things you don't know that are critical to your success, then you can endeavor to learn about those topics. You may even find it necessary to hire someone who is an expert in one or more of these topics. Some topics do require years of experience to become an expert, and you may not have the time to learn the subject with the necessary depth of knowledge. Again, Stinking Thinking can be your enemy. Do not be fooled into thinking that you or a team member are experts after reading a few articles on the subject matter. It usually takes years of hard work to become an expert.

Often, on the job, I was fond of admonishing people that "if you don't know what you don't know, you are dangerous."

This can apply to products, technology, competitors, management processes, financial procedures, and other areas of business. How you think about a particular subject depends upon the information in your brain. Be sure that your mental 'database' is up-to-date. You should always be scanning your environment for new information that is relevant to your work. In addition when you are in a meeting, be careful how you express your opinion on any given subject. There are topics, of course, in which you are an expert. On these topics you can act in a confident manner. But, if you have an opinion on a topic in which you are not an expert, please be careful to inform the meeting attendees that you may be wrong. Enlightened Thinking dictates that a little humility is very appropriate in those situations. In meetings, I would often share my opinion on a subject by first saying: "I could be wrong."

So right now, start making a list of what you don't know that is relevant to your work. It really is best if you are not a danger to your own team. Your company's success depends upon it!

PERSONAL APPLICATION

1) Am I too risk adverse?
2) Do I hire the best people?
3) Do I have a list of what I do not know, that I need to know?
4) Write down your Big Decision:

BE AGGRESSIVE

BE AT THE RIGHT PLACE AT THE RIGHT TIME

****

DIFFICULT CONVERSATIONS ARE VERY GOOD

****

DEMOLISH ROADBLOCKS

****

HIRE THE BEST PEOPLE

****

PUSH TECHNOLOGY – BUT ONLY SO FAR

****

KNOW WHAT YOU DON'T KNOW

SELF-TALK ON AGGRESSIVENESS

ADVANCED THOUGHT PLANNING:

AM I AT THE RIGHT PLACE?

DO I OFTEN AVOID CRITICAL TOPICS?

HOW CAN I BE SIMULTANEOUSLY AGGRESSIVE AND OPEN TO CRITICISM?

HAVE I CHALLENGED MY TEAM TO LIST WHAT WE DO NOT KNOW?

****

THE BIG DECISION:

I WILL PLAN WISELY, WITH CONFIDENCE, AND I WILL BE AGGRESSIVE

IT'S HALF TIME

TAKE SOME TIME TO THINK

You have now read about half of this book. I hope that you have learned that it is crucial to take time to dwell on Enlightened Thinking. And it's also crucial to become aware of your Stinking Thinking, and then eliminate it!

So, take 10 or 15 minutes right now in Advanced Thought Planning. Make the Big Decision, and write down a list of self-talk habits that you may need to consider changing.

Chapter Seven

Keep It Simple –
As Simple As Possible

———— ∞∞∞ ————

KEY POINT:

Always keep your products and your organization as simple as possible. It does make life more successful, and enjoyable.

STINKING THINKING:

I am not going to waste my time thinking about simplicity. I'm a busy person.

ENLIGHTENED THINKING:

Simplicity really does matter. I want to ensure that my business objectives are clear and impactful.

I love simplicity! Simplicity just makes everything easier. My friends often say that I'm a simple person. (I'll take that as a compliment.) In fact, when my self-talk becomes too complicated, I become physically and emotionally tired, very quickly. Albert Einstein was famously quoted as saying: "If you can't explain it to a six year old, you don't understand it yourself."

In my own experience, I have found that when someone really understands a given topic, they can explain it quickly and in a simple manner. It does take a great deal of understanding and insight to effectively communicate the essence of a given topic. On the other hand when someone rambles on at length to explain some topic to me, I begin to wonder if they really have a thorough understanding of the topic themselves. When my own thinking is concise and simple, that is when I can communicate clearly.

I have repeatedly found that simplicity is often the essence of Enlightened Thinking.

During my years in college, and even now, the subject of Physics has always appealed to me. Physics is all about the essence of the universe. It's amazing to me to be able to understand the essential basics of what makes something work the way it does. It's even more amazing to understand why something does not work. And, it's most amazing, when in business we can anticipate whether something will work or not! I've always found it to be very useful to think about the basics of what I'm trying to accomplish.

Usually success or failure can be attributed to really knowing the basics of your business.

But, there are topics that by their nature are complicated. For example, the organization chart of a 1,000 person company is not simple. However, don't make it more complicated than necessary. I've seen organization structures that are hopelessly contorted on paper and in real life. No one could understand how the company actually got work done, including the employees. I would like to devote some serious Advanced Thought Planning to the general topic of business structure.

BUILD SIMPLE ORGANIZATIONS

The first aspect of a business that is best kept simple is the organization's structure.

An organization should be lean and to the point.

For example, it's always best to maximize an organization's management ratio – meaning having the maximum number of employees led by as few managers as possible in that organization. Fewer managers will enable quicker decisions, fewer arguments, and lower personnel-related expenses. It is far too easy to allow an organization to grow with too many managers.

Our Stinking Thinking can often lead us toward placing more managers on our staff. We may think that more managers will give us the appearance of being more important.

In addition, we may think that more managers may even justify a salary increase for ourselves. If your self-talk trends in this direction, please, re-read the chapter on humility. You need to stop this Stinking Thinking!

Another strong influence that results in too many managers in an organization is employees who are too eager for a promotion. This desire for promotion is often the result of common, traditional Stinking Thinking. People often think that their careers are more successful when they receive a more flattering title. So, these employees will often push you for a promotion, and it's easy to quickly approve their request rather than engage in a needed difficult conversation. Resist the inclination to say "yes" to a promotion request, unless you really do need another manager.

By the way please don't be an employee who is too eager for a promotion. I know in my own experience that envy often triggered my Stinking Thinking. In my youth, it would hurt my pride if a fellow worker was promoted and not me. But, think about it. Focus your self-talk on what's best for the company, and try to maintain a humble attitude. Enlightened Thinking will lead you to congratulate a fellow employee when they are promoted.

To summarize the topic of maintaining fewer managers in an organization, I always tried to keep each manager's span of control to at least five direct reports, with a maximum of 10 direct reports. An organizational structure built with these numbers can enable great productivity and low cost. This large span of control also enables clearer responsibilities, as I will now discuss.

Another key structural principle is to design your organization so that responsibilities and the associated authorities are as clear as possible. Do your best to assign organizational names that are self-descriptive of what each organization actually does every day. Minimize any overlap in responsibilities. Feuding can often result if two people believe that they are both responsible for a particular decision. Each group's responsibility should be as obvious as possible, and when it's not obvious be sure to document everyone's authority and responsibility.

Do some Advanced Thought Planning and ask your team for suggestions on how to streamline workflows.

Listen to the feedback from your team. Do not be prideful. Always strive to be the champion of openness and simplicity.

Here's one last thought on organizational structures. When possible, I believe that it is best to try to somewhat under staff projects. Fewer people will translate into less communication overhead and less confusion. In general simpler is better when it comes to headcount. Unfortunately the frequent negative self-talk of many managers leads them to argue for additional people in their group. Their Stinking Thinking is to earn themselves a raise or a promotion through additional headcount.

Management pay scales are usually linked to their department's expenses or headcount. As a great leader in search of simplicity, you will need to say "no" at the proper time to hiring requests, in order to keep your organization efficient. Be mindful that it always seems easy to hire people today. However, if you over-staff your group, it will be very difficult to reduce the number of people at some point in the future. No one wants to be involved with the layoff of good, productive employees.

BUILD SIMPLE PRODUCTS

Products and services should also be kept as simple as possible. I love creativity, but there can be a tension between creativity and simplicity. If creativity leads to products with too many features, often called "feature-creep," this can be the enemy of low-cost and time-to-market. Here is another case where it may be necessary for you to say "no" to employees' suggestions that lead to complexity.

Through Advanced Thought Planning I believe that you will conclude that real creativity should lead to simplicity.

During the product definition and development stages, as features are added to a product, it is very difficult to track the product's total cost. Usually at the end of multiple discussions which repeatedly add features to the product, it's not uncommon for everyone to be negatively surprised when the costs are accurately reported to the team weeks later. Then it takes even more time to agree to remove features in an intelligent manner through even more meetings.

In addition everyone must realize that the product development elapsed time increases substantially as more features are included in the development phase of the product. All of this feature-creep further delays the introduction of the product, and the revenue that was expected from the product shipments is also delayed. The necessary Advanced Thought Planning is: adding too many features to a new product is really a very bad idea. Of course the necessary Enlightened Thinking is: keep it simple.

The proper definition of a creative product is one that is simple and yet is extremely useful.

We need to readjust our self-talk to creatively think about simplicity. Of course, the best approach to product definition is to know your potential customers. Don't be fooled into the Stinking Thinking that you know your customer's needs better than they do themselves. You should proactively identify key, knowledgeable customers and visit with them, arriving with an open mind. Your self-talk should avoid jumping to conclusions. Let your customers be your guide.

You should also have a clear idea of 'why' these customers will buy your product or service. You should clearly know how much these customers are willing to pay for your product or service. The benefits and costs for your customers, should be well understood by your team. Ask key customers to help you understand their reasoning and product purchasing criteria. You may want to challenge your team to spend a lot more time with key customers. When I was working at Xilinx, we had agreed that all senior managers would meet with at least five key customers every quarter.

In addition, when planning your product portfolio, you should have a solid understanding of your future competition. Your product must exceed your customer's expectations, as set by their real needs, while you are being mindful of your competitor's product offering. But, avoid the naive self-talk that arrogantly concludes that your competitor can't improve their current product. It's best to expect that your competition will improve their offering.

So, be sure to exceed your customer's current expectations but not by too much of a margin. Keep in mind that too many added features will raise your costs and delay the product's introduction into the market. If your competitors overshoot the customer's needs, you don't necessarily have to follow them and make the same mistake. You can offer your product at a lower price. But of course, if you set your price too low you are making a different mistake and unnecessarily reducing your profitability.

It is always exciting to try to dominate a market with the lowest price, but you should make sure that you understand the associated impact to your business. Sometimes it's smarter to aim for a 60 percent market share, and still be the number one player in the market, rather than trying to garner an 80 percent market share and totally dominate the market.

If you are sacrificing a high gross margin for that market domination, it's probably best to rethink your pricing strategy. Don't let prideful self-talk lead you on an ego trip toward market domination. Wall Street will reward you more for keeping your gross margins respectably high. Wall Street will not pay you for a large ego. The best way to attain an impressive market capitalization is to be the industry market share leader, and also deliver high gross margins.

Finally keep in mind, that after you have introduced your product into the market, it's always possible to launch a more featured product at a later date. Apple Inc. is an absolute expert at utilizing this strategy, for example, with the iPhone product family. This strategy has allowed them to defend themselves against low-cost competition while adding sophisticated features over time, to actually raise the customer's expectations.

Apple has been able to bring products to market quickly and on a regular basis. Their competition has not been able to execute effectively against this strategy. You must be careful, however, about adding more features to an existing product. More features can lead to a product that is difficult to use. I have often been amazed that customers may prefer a simpler product that offers better ease of use characteristics. But once again, Apple is masterful at providing sophisticated features and excellent ease of use.

Defining a world-class product does require extensive Advanced Thought Planning by a team of experienced experts! I believe that this aspect of your company is the most challenging activity you will undertake. Do be very careful with your product definition. If you try to serve too many diverse needs with a single product, you may wind up serving no market very well. There must be a balance between features, ease of use, and product cost.

CHOSE A SIMPLE TECHNOLOGY

Your company's use of technology should be kept as simple as is possible. This approach to the use of technology will give you a much higher probability of success.

Through careful Advanced Thought Planning, you should conclude that there is no point in taking additional business risk, if you can accomplish your business goals with a technology that is already well understood.

I believe that many start-up companies in Silicon Valley have failed because the founders underestimated the technical challenges that they were undertaking with their product plans. In many cases, it was not necessary to be so aggressive with the technology, but engineer's egos can often push them to the 'bleeding edge' (beyond the 'cutting edge') of technology for bragging rights at dinner meetings. This is the ultimate bad example of Stinking Thinking because it causes expensive, unnecessary failure. Unfortunately, this type of negative self-talk is very, very common.

For example in today's semiconductor technology, it is possible to implement very complex circuits with 65 nanometer design rules. These circuits are relatively easy to design using that technology, and the manufacturing costs are very low. However, many new companies are, instead trying to design their products with more difficult and expensive 28 nanometer design rules, even though they could successfully bring their product to market with less aggressive design rules. It's always best to minimize the technical risks in order to maximize your probability of success. Please, do not let your ego overrule Enlightened Thinking. Keep it simple.

If it really is necessary to be dramatically aggressive with technology, be sure that you and your team are experts in that technology. Make sure that you know what you don't know! And, add time into your product schedules for the unexpected problems that are sure to arise during development. It's never easy to be one of the early users of any technology. A great deal of Advanced Thought Planning is required.

I would encourage you to properly estimate the risks before proceeding on the 'bleeding edge' of technology. If you do succeed on the 'bleeding edge,' you will have earned those associated bragging rights over dinner. But if you fail because you underestimated the complexity of the technology, you will feel very disappointed with yourself, and you may have consumed a great deal of money in the process. If you fail, I predict that your self-talk will become very negative!

In the early stages of your company's existence, maybe you should consider some other less risky business venture that would be better to pursue with your available resources and time. Once your business is launched and you are spending money with a specific strategy, it's very difficult psychologically to stop or change what you are doing, despite the mounting evidence of underestimated risk. We humans find it very difficult to admit when we are wrong. This is also a very common form of Stinking Thinking.

SIMPLIFY OVERALL OBJECTIVES

Finally as you pursue your dream of success, if your business endeavor becomes more and more complicated, don't start counting on too many 'miracles' to keep your business and career successful. "Keep it Simple, Stupid" (KISS), could be the best advice you have ever heard.

Business is tough enough without trying to accomplish the seemingly impossible.

A key question to periodically ask yourself is: has my dream become far too complicated, and is it unlikely to succeed? If the answer is "no," proceed with assurance. If the answer is "maybe," only proceed after you have completed a thorough inventory of all of the breakthroughs that are necessary to assure success. As you ask yourself this question, be very careful about your self-talk. It is very easy to fool yourself and not conduct a thorough business analysis.

Make sure that you and your team are also reading material that may be critical of your business choices. Because of Stinking Thinking, we may absent-mindedly avoid negative topics associated with our work. We really do not like to admit that we may have made a mistake. In order to maximize the probability of success, analyze the work to determine if you can further simplify your endeavor.

If your business analysis reveals that you need only one major breakthrough, success is possible, but not highly probable. If you require two or more breakthroughs, stop what you are doing now. You must find a way to simplify what you are attempting to accomplish. You may find it useful to re-read the discussion about taking too much risk located in Chapter Six. There may be a better alternative place for you to be in business at this point in time. I know that it is wonderfully exhilarating to be aggressive, but it's also very easy to get foolishly carried away with your dreams.

LIVE A SIMPLE LIFE

I can't help suggesting that simplicity is also wonderful in your daily life. The world has become enamored with acquiring money and things, but little do we realize how these activities complicate living. Everything we own requires time and maintenance; soon we become slaves to our own possessions.

We need to, constantly, ask ourselves how we can attain true satisfaction in life.

Do not let your Stinking Thinking lead you into the trap of 'more is better.' Hollywood, internet advertisements, and television commercials would seem to indicate that we always need more stuff. They certainly want all of us to buy more stuff! Our social existence has become an incessant advertising experience. It is like fish living in a polluted pond. Even after a relatively short period of time, these fish can't even recognize the pollution.

If we are being told, hundreds of times each day that 'more is better,' soon we may believe that falsehood. Even if we do not agree with the fantasy, we can be strongly influenced, unconsciously, by the continuous hype bombarding our minds. However, the concept of 'more is better' is simply not true.

Please, do some serious Advanced Thought Planning on the subject of what is true satisfaction for you and your family. Once you have answered that question, then, you can know that everything else will become a distraction without satisfaction. Enlightened Thinking dictates that, even in our daily life, we should know that simplicity will give us the best opportunity to fulfill our dreams.

PERSONAL APPLICATION

1) Am I enthusiastically pursuing simplicity?
2) Are my organizational responsibilities clear and well documented?
3) Can we simplify our product technology?
4) Write down your Big Decision:

KEEP 'IT' SIMPLE

KISS

✳✳✳✳

**KEEP 'IT' SIMPLE; AT LEAST AS SIMPLE
AS POSSIBLE**

✳✳✳✳

**'IT' INCLUDES ORGANIZATIONS,
PRODUCTS, TECHNOLOGY, AND LIFE**

✳✳✳✳

**CREATIVITY: SIMPLICITY PLUS
USEFULNESS**

SELF-TALK on SIMPLICITY

ADVANCED THOUGHT PLANNING:

HOW DO I BUILD AN EFFECTIVE ORGANIZATION?

CAN OUR PRODUCTS BE SIMPLER?

IS MY PRIDE LINKED TO OUR TECHNOLOGY?

HAS MY DREAM BECOME TOO COMPLICATED?

✳✳✳✳

THE BIG DECISION:

I WILL PURSUE SIMPLICITY; A SIMPLER LIFE IS BETTER

Chapter Eight

Focus - And Focus Again

––––––∞∞∞––––––

KEY POINT:
Focus is crucial to get things done quickly and successfully; it is often necessary to say "no" to distractions.

STINKING THINKING:
I do not need to plan my workday. In fact, it can be fun. What's the big deal anyway?

ENLIGHTENED THINKING:
My time, and my team's time, is extremely valuable. We must plan our day wisely.

To be successful you must be productive. It's necessary that on a daily basis you and your team accomplish pre-defined goals. Then, after many days and many months, these accumulated daily accomplishments will yield successful business results. The only way to get things done daily is to be focused every day on your objectives. (In Chapter Nine we will discuss how to set and measure clear objectives.)

I believe that focus is achieved by saying "no," at the right time, to anything that can distract you from your objectives. That sounds a bit strange, but I believe it's true.

The bottom line is that we need to do Advanced Thought Planning in order to minimize distractions in our work environment.

We need to avoid the Stinking Thinking that leads us to unconsciously conclude that productivity is unimportant. For example, if you are busy getting your work completed, and someone interrupts you with a college basketball score, it's very tempting to check out your teams last play on the internet. Or more seriously, if you are busy developing a product for one market, and someone brings you an interesting new idea for another market, you have a decision to make at that juncture. I believe that you have to decide to say "no," with a positive attitude. You have to remain focused on the task at hand, until it is completed. Of course you also want to be polite and get back to that person with their new idea when the time is right. Through Advanced Thought Planning, I decided to keep a 'parking lot' of new ideas that may be worth pursuing at some future date, but only after I had finished with the current work. In fact, my current work was likely a new idea from the recent past. Write down the new, great idea in your 'parking lot' using a piece of paper or a computer file.

At Xilinx I kept a 'parking lot' file on my laptop. I often shared this list with fellow engineers as they approached me with more, new ideas. I would assure these creative engineers that we would revisit their ideas at the right time in the future. Of course, I also let them know that we had dozens of other great ideas in the 'parking lot.' Their new idea did have competition. That was a great situation for the company! We had many, many new ideas waiting to be pursued in the future. However, I made sure that it was clear to everyone involved, that for the time being, we had the current project to finish.

Going one step further in Advanced Thought Planning, it would be most productive to build an office environment which inherently limits your interruptions. Put in place a plan that maximizes productivity. When you are involved in deep thinking, put up a sign at the door of your cubical that says: "Please do NOT interrupt." Also have a method to turn off your phone during these time periods. Keep in mind that if you are interrupted once in an hour, for only five minutes, it then requires several minutes to resume your original thought pattern, and you have lost 15 percent of your productivity! In fact, a recent study of software engineers found that they only spend an average of eleven minutes on one task, before they are interrupted to deal with another activity.[14] That is a loss of productivity in excess of 50 percent. Interruptions can certainly be very expensive.

JUST SAY "NO"

This chapter is all about learning to say "no" to distractions. Now, doesn't that sound nice and simple? But, it's not easy to do for the typical human being.

Life is full of distractions and enticements; as a result, we have to learn to say "no."

I believe that this is a learned skill. Our Stinking Thinking can lead us to politely allow others to interrupt our work. Our self-talk will lead us to allow people to distract us because we want to be liked. We certainly don't want to offend a fellow worker. It's a choice we need to make. What is your Big Decision? Will you build a plan to manage interruptions that reduce your productivity? We all need to learn how to set appropriate boundaries: we need to periodically turn off our email; we need to periodically turn off our cell phones; we need to periodically turn off the internet; and so on.

There is another, even more insidious mechanism, which detracts from our focus. Do we aggressively manage our own self-talk? I'm even more prone to let my own thoughts interrupt my focus on the work at hand. For example, even as I'm writing this book, my thoughts drift toward the state of the stock market. I wonder if the market is going up or down this afternoon. One of the differences between a child and a mature adult is in the ability to focus on what is really important and ignore everything else. So be an adult and don't tolerate sloppy thought habits. Each of us must learn to live our daily lives with discipline.

In summary, there are two great distractions to being focused: other people and myself.

In fact the entire world around us can be the enemy of focus. In a leadership role, focus can be especially difficult because we are surrounded by very smart employees who believe that, in addition to what we are now doing at our work, more things can and should be done as well. Our manager and our customers are always going to ask us to do more.

Smart people, including you, have many good ideas. But successful leaders pick out the best ideas, and then stay focused long enough to be successful. Focus means sticking with the most important tasks; no jumping around is allowed until success is secure. Disciplined self-talk really does matter in business and in life. Make your Big Decision right now.

SET CLEAR GOALS

One of the best ways to successfully say "no" to distractions is to know what to say "yes" to each day. Through Advanced Thought Planning, each person in an organization should have documented clear goals for this year, this quarter, this week, and today. The annual goals should comprise no more than 10 items, with the top three clearly identified for emphasis. These goals should be as quantified as possible so that at the end of the year they can be measured by you and your manager. The quarterly and weekly goals should be limited to at most three items, of course based upon the annual goals. The goals for today should be limited to one or two items.

The first thing I do in the morning is to write down what my focus is for today. I write down those one or two items that will get done today, for sure! I then take that piece of paper and stick it in my pocket as a constant reminder to keep me focused. These items can also be placed into a laptop or PDA screen saver as a reminder. Then as the day unfolds, and I'm distracted by some urgent interruption, the piece of paper reminds me to quickly get back to my focus items. Day after day, it requires a constant vigilance to stay focused and as a result be successful. I believe that the frequent Stinking Thinking in this area is simply laziness. Managers usually fail to recognize just how critical it is to establish these daily goals. True leaders take the time to think through these goals, and as a result avoid wasting many hours every day through a multiplicity of distractions.

It's even more important to keep the key annual and quarterly organizational goals visible to all of the employees. Proactively help every person in your organization remain focused. Use any technique necessary to help keep you and others properly focused on the key goals. These techniques could include posters, web pages, and emails. Bumper stickers can be very useful as 'sticky' reminders for employees. It's very useful to boil down a key goal to a few words, so it's easy to remember and fits on a bumper sticker.

If you can't capture a key goal in a few words, maybe you need to really think about the essence of that goal. Or, it's possible that you need to identify a better, simpler key goal that will lead you to success. A simple description is the best way to ensure that the entire team fully understands what is being achieved through their work.

You may have heard of the old story of two stonecutters who were laboring side by side in the quarry on a very hot day. One was highly motivated because he knew that he was working on a stone that would be part of a great cathedral. The other was bored and listless because he was cutting just another stone without the goal of the cathedral in his 'mind's eye.' How we think can not only change our perspective, but also our productivity. The proper definition of organizational goals, and linked personal goals, can lead to highly motivated focused people. Encourage all of your fellow employees to do the Advanced Thought Planning needed to clearly establish their own daily goals.

BE SPECIAL

A 'funny' thing happens as you sharpen your focus; you become special. You can become the best at whatever you do, if you focus your thinking and your energy on your specialty. If what you do is valuable in the world's marketplace (see Chapter Six: "Be At The Right Place At The Right Time"), and you are the best at what you do; then you have a great chance of being successful. This can apply to an individual or to an entire company.

Success is all about choosing a valuable specialization, which leads to excellence.

Enlightened Thinking will cause us to work diligently toward the goal of being an expert. Most people, through Stinking Thinking, believe that it's valuable to be a 'jack of all trades.' But, in most cases, that's just not true. In our highly complex world, most people can't excel in many disciplines simultaneously. These people may get a false sense of security by attempting to be a 'jack of all trades.' Usually this self-talk is delusional. This Stinking Thinking often becomes an excuse to be lazy. It's very easy to think that you're a 'jack of all trades' when in fact you are a 'jack of no trade.' These folks further believe that if they get laid off by their current employer, then they will more easily be able to find another job with their broad skills. However, I believe that it would be best for them to focus on retaining their current job by being an expert, rather than planning for a potential release from their current job. In this modern world it's usually the experts who are retained, promoted, and highly paid.

For yourself and for your company, pick a valuable focus and become an expert. If in the course of time, it turns out that your specialization is no longer in demand, then plan to switch to a new specialty. The switch will take some time, so be sure to anticipate this requirement by a year or two. I believe that this approach to specialization will give you the highest probability of success in your career. Obviously, your career choice is crucial. Please do give a great deal of quality Advanced Thought Planning to this topic. What is your Big Decision?

PRIORITIZE RESOURCES

The need for focus includes your time and energy, and, it also includes all of your resources. If you are employed as a manager, I'm sure that the resources at your disposal far exceed the value of your own personal time. These resources include all the people that you influence, plus money, equipment, etc. Are your resources focused?

Are you managing all of these resources in a manner consistent with your key goals?

Can you specifically answer that crucial question? There is only one way to really be able to give an appropriate answer: you must ask yourself if you are measuring the effectiveness of your resource deployment. You have to check, and verify through measurement techniques, that your resources are deployed where you really want them to be utilized each day.

Enlightened Thinking dictates that leaders set the tempo and speed of an organization. For example, effective military generals know where their troops are today and where they will be tomorrow. A leader determines the troop deployment. Battles are fought and won through focused resource deployment. As leaders we need to do some serious Advanced Thought Planning.

On a quarterly basis I found it to be a useful exercise to look at the size of each of my organizations, and ensure that they were scaled to our business priorities. It's easy to have one group of people grow too quickly through rapid hiring, while another group grows slowly through careful hiring; only picking the few outstanding candidates that they were able to interview. It's up to you as the responsible manager to keep your organizations in proper balance based upon the critical goals.

Of course, it's also important to verify that the resources that the company has entrusted to you are actually achieving these critical goals. Enlightened Thinking will lead us as managers to do periodic checking. I often found it useful to ask other employees, especially my direct reporting managers, what their top goal was for this current week. As I was walking into our cafeteria, it was always a great conversation starter to simply ask someone about their top priority. By doing this in a friendly way, you convey that you care about that person, and that you care about the company as well. Effective generals need to visit the front lines periodically, and ask the troops about their activities.

At HP this practice was commonly referred to as management by walking around. These conversations can then easily move into a discussion of the progress that is being achieved toward your goals. Hopefully, everything is proceeding according to the established plan. If not, it's very gratifying to ask if you can help in some way; the person will feel very encouraged and may even accept your offer for assistance. Enlightened Thinking is very contagious.

All too often during these conversations with 'the troops,' I would discover that people did not perceive the same priorities that I had assumed were agreed to by the management team. At that point, I found that it was best to jot down a note to myself, and I would speak to that person's manager later in private in order to resolve the situation. Sometimes it was a simple misunderstanding, but more often I found that the manager and I did not really agree on the goals. I had been assuming that there was agreement across the entire team. Enlightened Thinking leads us to do some checking.

Stinking Thinking is usually lazy and leads us to make, possible, false assumptions.

Management by walking around was an opportunity to make sure that our resources had been properly prioritized across the organization.

Another technique for focus that worked very well at Xilinx was our 'all employees' quarterly update meeting. I would simply spend one hour with various groups of engineers to discuss the results of our key projects from the past quarter and the key goals for the new quarter. This was a superb method to ensure that everyone across the organization had a clear direction. After every one of these meetings, at least one person would chat with me about the presentation, because they thought there were different priorities. This is a wonderful way to clear the air and resolve the different opinions that will certainly exist within any group of people. These quarterly meetings did take a lot of planning. Advanced Thought Planning does take time, but it is worth the resulting focus and productivity.

PERSONAL APPLICATION

1) Why don't I say "no" when it is appropriate?
2) Are my goals for today clear?
3) Do I fear specialization?
4) Write down your Big Decision:

<u>FOCUS</u>

FOCUS BY SAYING "NO,"

WITH A POSITIVE ATTITUDE

****

WHAT'S YOUR GOAL TODAY?

****

SPECIALIZE UNTIL YOU'RE SPECIAL

****

PRIORITIZE RESOURCES

****

MANAGE BY WALKING AROUND

SELF-TALK on FOCUS

ADVANCED THOUGHT PLANNING:

HOW WILL I SAY "NO?"

WHAT ARE MY GOALS?

WHAT IS MY SPECIALTY?

****

THE BIG DECISION:

I WILL SAY "NO"

I WILL SPECIALIZE

Chapter Nine

Measure It - or Don't Do It

---∞∞∞---

KEY POINT:
In business and in life, set goals that can be measured, so you can know for sure that you are making progress.

STINKING THINKING:
I am too busy to measure my team's activities. Anyway, everything is fine, as far as I know.

ENLIGHTENED THINKING:
Our work activities are valuable. Let's take the time to measure our progress toward key goals.

In a business environment, if there is something worth doing, then it should be important to the results that you expect from your endeavor. And, if it is an important activity, then you had better know how you will verify progress toward these results during that activity.

The classic example of a poorly managed project is one that will require many years to complete with no one effectively checking on valid intermediate milestones. When the project winds up a year late, with poor quality, and way over budget, everyone seems surprised by the negative results. Apparently no one thought that measuring progress was important. This sloppy management team actually got the results that they should have anticipated at the start of this project.

The Stinking Thinking of sloppy managers usually revolves around either arrogance or inexperience. Arrogance will take the form of self-talk that repeatedly claims: "I know what I'm doing; I don't need someone checking on me." Or, the inexperienced manager will simply not think about the need for measurements and clear goals. Have these thoughts shown up in your thinking?

Unfortunately, early in my career I fell victim to both forms of Stinking Thinking! Over time I did switch to Enlightened Thinking. I learned that a well-managed activity should include a detailed status report, documented on a monthly basis. I also learned that meaningful intermediate milestones should be defined at the beginning of a project. Then, as the project proceeds, there should be red flags raised by the team if these intermediate milestones are running behind schedule.

I've also noticed that managers who don't set well defined goals will usually also not appropriately delegate responsibility and authority. In their self-talk, they fear correctly that they will not be able to track the progress of the project unless they retain the authority for themselves. This leads to micromanagement and frustration for everyone. Unfortunately, despite the attempted micromanagement, these managers will probably not be able to accurately track the project's progress. One person simply can't really know whether or not a project is on schedule. Overall, this is a very ineffective way to manage an organization.

START RIGHT

I believe that the key to organizing a successful project is extensive preparation at the start of the various activities. Early in a project, Advanced Thought Planning is absolutely necessary.

Experienced people know, that getting started in an organized fashion, will lead to the appropriate management discipline over the length of the project.

When you start an activity in an undisciplined manner, psychologically it's very difficult to later stop and put the proper methodology in place. As I discussed before, many people do not like to admit that they made a mistake and change direction. If your Stinking Thinking prohibited the proper approach to measurable objectives, then that same Stinking Thinking will prohibit you from recognizing the need to later stop and correct your mistake.

Our arrogant self-talk is extremely habitual. That is why, when serious troubles arise on a project, it's usually necessary to hire or transfer a new manager into the project, to quickly change to the proper management methodology. Sometimes, the only way to change someone's thinking and behavior, is to fire them.

At the beginning of a project, the team should document the key goals in a manner that permits direct, easy measurement of those goals. The document should be placed under change control by the senior management. During the course of the project, before any goal is modified or rescheduled, key players in the team should be required to approve the change in writing.

Enlightened Thinking dictates that changes should include a review by many team members, in order to avoid wishful thinking.

By the way, as schedule changes occur in the project, it's also useful to check that the resulting product or service will still be a great success when it's completed as originally intended by the company. For example, it's not unusual during a long project for costs to increase, and it's possible that the product is no longer going to be price competitive. It's mandatory that product costs are tracked in detail as the project proceeds toward completion.

In addition during a long project, your competition could unexpectedly introduce a new product that directly undermines your product. You must keep your mind open to the need for possible changes in your plans.

CONDUCT 'REAL' STATUS REVIEWS

Once the project is launched, monthly status reviews should be conducted with key team members in attendance. It is critical to hold monthly meetings.

Frequent reviews will ensure that delayed milestones can't be ignored, and monthly reviews will facilitate quick reaction to issues as they arise.

Progress reports should be presented with clarity and include a great amount of measurable, factual data. These meetings must be conducted with an open and honest attitude; everyone must be 'real.' If the project is on schedule, then there is reason for celebration. But if schedules are being missed for some reason, then these facts must be discussed with recovery plans agreed to by the team.

Tough and intelligent questions must be encouraged, and directly answered before proceeding to other topics. Stinking Thinking may cause team members to attempt to avoid bad news at these monthly reviews. All too often these types of meetings become a 'feel good' show, and people become defensive when tough questions are raised. If this atmosphere becomes prevalent, the project is doomed at that point. When negative facts are being hidden or avoided, it becomes impossible to identify a recovery plan.

As a leader, one of your responsibilities is to encourage Enlightened Thinking. Everyone should be open and honest, especially with negative results or disappointing information. One of the best ways to encourage openness is to set the correct example, as we discussed in Chapter Four.

Always remember that people are watching how you handle tough questions or the reporting of negative results.

If you react in a defensive emotional manner to poor reported results, people will stop making those reports. The results may continue to be poor in reality, but you will not hear about that reality. Or, if your reaction to a tough question is to ignore it, or even worse to disparage the questioner, then people will simply stop asking those appropriate tough questions.

Smart managers always want to really know what is going on, at the battlefield level. You must encourage an open flow of information. Through early Advanced Thought Planning, speak with the team members at the beginning of the project. Explain how critical it is that the monthly reviews be open and honest. It's easiest to have that conversation at the beginning of the project, because, at that time no one is behind schedule, yet.

FIX IT NOW

Always keep in mind that it's best to solve a problem as early as possible. If people are trying to hide their problem thinking that they will resolve the issue before management can discover it, then they are setting things up for possible failure by postponing the real problem resolution.

In an open environment where people trust each other, they quickly look to the team for help.

The manager's attitude toward discussing issues will determine how people handle the flow of critical information. For example, the classic debugging scenario in software projects involves finding and fixing bugs after the source code has been written. Software engineers will often avoid reporting bugs in their own code, in order to avoid the necessity to explain "why" that bug occurred in their code. Their Stinking Thinking leads them to secrecy, in order to avoid possible embarrassment. But, by sharing the cause of a bug with peers, it's often possible to find many other existing bugs in the source code, due to the exact same cause.

Often, engineers also want to avoid peer code reviews for the same reasons. However, it costs over 1,000 times more to fix a bug reported by a customer then if the programmers find that same bug in a code review procedure before the product is shipped to customers.[15] Enlightened Thinking dictates that peers can help find and resolve problems early, if each team member is willing to accept help from one another. Strong teams focus on Enlightened Thinking, and helping one another, instead of dwelling in selfish Stinking Thinking. Where does your team spend most of their time? As a leader, you must think about these issues of self-talk!

The bottom line is to manage in a manner that will encourage the identification and open discussion of problems. That approach to project management will identify problems early, and allow for a rapid resolution of the problem. The whole purpose of monthly status reviews is to report issues and then to ensure that they are resolved quickly.

In addition, I've also found it useful to have private one-hour meetings every two weeks with each person on my staff. These meetings allowed us to catch up on the project's status, and discuss possible problems before they became acute. These private meetings also allowed us to discuss the need for Enlightened Thinking to pervade every aspect of our management style.

LEARN FROM MISTAKES

Finally, it is possible to gauge the quality of a team by the number of problems that are reported by customers, after delivery of the product. For example, an excellent team who has many years of experience together, doing similar projects, will have fewer reported problems. They will simply make fewer mistakes because they have the appropriate experience. In particular, they have learned from their past mistakes and Stinking Thinking, and they are able to deliver a successful project more efficiently through Enlightened Thinking.

Each of their successive projects should demonstrate a learning ability, and growth in effective results.

On the other hand, if your team is experiencing a large number of problems and doesn't seem to be learning from their mistakes, then you must take action. It may be necessary to take some time out of the project for special intense training. Or, it may be necessary to bring into the project some managers with much more experience. Product development teams should always strive to improve their productivity and quality.

You as a manager must be very careful how you react to this particular problem reporting metric. It's very easy for team members to stop reporting problems, if they perceive that management is penalizing people for honestly reporting the problems that customers encounter.

As a manager you must react to poor results, but only in a fashion that is perceived as being fair and effective by the team members.

Problems are often the result of someone habitually not properly performing their job. Stinking Thinking is habitual. In order to improve our products at Xilinx, a question I often asked the team was: "Who has to change what behavior?"

But of course, when asking the question, it's best to avoid sounding too onerous.

In general, inexperienced teams will resist documenting goals, conducting monthly reviews, and reporting problems. Inexperienced people will often view these activities as unnecessary overhead and a waste of time. The reality is that these activities are overhead. But it's your job to convince people that this overhead is absolutely necessary for a successful project, and for efficient learning on the job.

If goals are not documented, they can be forgotten or misunderstood a few months later. If monthly reviews are not conducted effectively, no one can really know if the project is on schedule. And if problems are not reported, they will most likely not get thoroughly fixed in a rapid fashion. In fact, the easiest way to check on the maturity of a team is to watch how wholeheartedly they react to setting goals and measuring their monthly results.

BUILD QUALITY

Excellence is achieved by building proper team habits! You and your team must focus on Enlightened Thinking.

Quality in your product is the result of repeatedly following well defined processes with clear documented goals.

Quality is never an accident; it is a habit. Successful teams will by habit encourage each other to follow the documented procedures. In fact it is critical, that your Advanced Thought Planning includes the generation of documented procedures.

Shortcuts to results very often wind up in a 'ditch.' Just a few years ago, I recall acquiring a company that seemingly possessed a new high-speed communication technology. The employees had a great deal of university knowledge, but very little actual development experience. They committed to deliver a product with the highest speed in the industry in a very short time frame.

To make a very long, painful story short, the product never did work in a reliable fashion under varying temperature conditions. We later learned that due to the team's inexperience, their testing procedures were woefully abbreviated in order to fulfill their aggressive schedule. Their Stinking Thinking was infested with arrogance. They did not conduct open monthly project reviews, and they purposefully hid embarrassing information.

I should have monitored their product development practices in much more detail. I should have inspected their procedures, in order to get what I expected from that team. My Stinking Thinking was wishful thinking! We and our customers suffered with poor quality products for several years, as a result of this failure.

The Japanese dramatically improved quality within their industrial complex over the past 50 years by simply establishing thorough operational habits that led to predictable, high-quality results. They also understood that there is a need to innovate and improve these work processes. But, they understood that these innovations must also be managed properly, as they are newly deployed into a workforce.

In my experience, unfortunately, I've seen too many American impetuous engineers introducing supposed innovations in a sloppy, ill–thought-out fashion. The result is usually a significant deterioration of quality, which can persist for a surprisingly long period of time. Unintended consequences are always a possibility, unless we carefully think through the implications of innovations before they are implemented by a workforce.

Of course we are all aware that the Japanese approach to quality has given them a clear lead in the automotive market. This management approach that employs careful, consistent measurement of progress towards documented, well-established goals often yields the best results over the long term. Japanese managers often engage in extensive Advanced Thought Planning when it comes to quality.

Because I live and work in Silicon Valley, I often observe the naive, short-term mindset that leads to 'one too many' shortcuts during the development of a new product. I believe that this is one of the key reasons why so many start-up companies end in failure.

I find it interesting that many Americans are inclined toward arrogant Stinking Thinking. Maybe our past success has negatively impacted our self-talk, and we erroneously believe that we don't need to carefully plan our endeavors. Maybe that same self-talk has also infiltrated the Japanese auto manufacturer Toyota. As a company their success had been legendary until they encountered recent quality issues. Human self-talk can easily go astray, especially when we have been very successful. We must be diligent. If we consistently exercise the principles of Measure It - or Don't Do It, we will be much better off in the long term.

PERSONAL APPLICATION

1) Am I guilty of wishful thinking in my self-talk?
2) Have I set clear, measurable goals for my team?
3) Does my team avoid accountability?
4) Write down your Big Decision:

<u>MEASURE IT –
OR DON'T DO IT</u>

INSPECT TO GET WHAT YOU EXPECT

****

THE PROJECT START IS KEY:

WHAT WILL YOU MEASURE?

****

MEASURE TWICE – CUT ONCE

THINK TWICE – ERROR LESS

****

**LEARN FROM MISTAKES
QUICKLY!**

SELF-TALK on MEASURE IT

ADVANCED THOUGHT PLANNING:

WHY AM I INCLINED TO AVOID ACCOUNTABILITY?

HOW CAN I ENCOURAGE OPEN & HONEST REVIEWS?

****

THE BIG DECISION:

TODAY I WILL SET CLEAR MEASURABLE GOALS FOR TODAY, THIS QUARTER, AND THIS YEAR

Chapter Ten

A Company Is Only As Good As The People

---⊶∞⊷---

KEY POINT:

Always remember that people are your company's most valuable resource; and that definitely includes you.

STINKING THINKING:

These people at work are a pain in my neck. They just don't get it! When will they wise up like me?

ENLIGHTENED THINKING:

I and my teammates need to grow on the job. We need to learn, together, the most effective work disciplines.

A t the end of a workday when all of the employees have gone home, what resources of your company are left behind? Basically, there is nothing of real value left behind. Oh sure there are buildings, equipment, and in some cases intellectual property left behind, but without intelligent dedicated people the company is not worth much at all. In fact, intelligent people were required to build those buildings, buy that equipment, and design the intellectual property.

The bottom line is that a company's most important resource is the people.

Even a little Advanced Thought Planning would lead to the conclusion that people are the most important asset! So doesn't it make sense that this resource should be treated with great care, in terms of nurturing these people and hiring even more, competent people?

To emphatically make this point at Xilinx, our Founder and CEO Bernie Vonderschmitt designed an organization chart that put him at the bottom of the sheet, and all of the employees were at the top of the organization chart. We posted these inverted organization charts in all of the conference rooms, to make sure that everyone remembered that they were the key to the success of the company.

Bernie knew how to daily impact our self-talk with Enlightened Thinking. This mindset propelled Xilinx to an $8 billion market capitalization by 2006. But, what was even more impressive, was that Xilinx and our employees were ranked in *Fortune* magazine's "Ten Best Places to Work" for four consecutive years! As a team we celebrated in our mutual success both emotionally and financially.

My own Enlightened Thinking, as a member of a team, must focus on the team.

As a leader I need to think about ways in which I can make all of my teammates more effective.

Of course, as discussed in Chapter Six, I should ask my teammates for their suggestions on how I can be more helpful to them on the job. As a manager, Enlightened Thinking becomes even more crucial for the company's success. People are relying on you and me to help them develop improved skills and be successful. Let's explore a number of possibilities.

EMPLOY TRAINING PROGRAMS

All of the services and products of any company are generated by people. These people require training, motivating, and they deserve rewards for great work.

Since a company is only as good as the employees, it is a necessary corollary that a company can only improve if the people improve.

Each person should be challenged to grow and develop on their job. Through Enlightened Thinking you should set the example in this area! Ask yourself: "How are you striving to improve?" Do people around you perceive that you are interested in growing in your skills? Don't get mislead by Stinking Thinking that purports that you don't need to grow. People will react badly to a prideful manager who thinks that only the employees are in need of training.

Training programs are absolutely necessary for everyone. Certainly newly hired people should take basic classes. And, there should be advanced classes available for more experienced employees. But training is much more than just classes.

As a manager you should also ensure that each employee has an effective mentor.

Be sure to select these mentors with great care; their approach to work will become highly influential. And that's exactly the point of assigning mentors; these mentors become the role models in your organization. A mentor can ensure that what a new employee learns from a class will be appropriately applied in everyday work situations. The best way for new employees to learn is on the job, with a great deal of practice and the guidance of a mentor.

However, even those who have been on their job for many years also need training. My own Stinking Thinking often resulted in me avoiding formal training. At that time, not only did I stop learning, but I also set a poor example for my teammates. Sometimes people can get stale on their job and new ideas simply stop occurring, or, new ideas are even resisted by that employee. It's often a very good idea to speak with these folks to find out if it may be a good time for a change in job assignment.

Every employee, including you and me, should have a mentor. If someone has been on their job for a long time, the mentor can suggest new approaches to the work. Or the mentor can provide coaching and encourage the person to move into a new position when that's appropriate. Mentors can provide the impetus for growth and development across your whole organization.

Let's try to do more Advanced Thought Planning in this critical area of training. We have to avoid the Stinking Thinking that leads to training being viewed as a secondary program. Unfortunately, the reality is that in most companies training classes are ineffective, boring, and de-motivating. Despite these numerous problems, management will usually "say" that these training classes are very important! As a manager we need to behave consistent with our values.

It's most appropriate to put one of your top employees in charge of periodically reviewing classes, to ensure that they are effective and motivating.

All classes and teachers should receive student grading with suggestions for improvement. It is important to measure the effectiveness of these training programs. Also, remember to be sure that you are setting the proper example when it comes to training. Are you taking classes periodically? Are you working as a mentor to another employee? Do you have a mentor to help you grow on the job?

STRIVE TO MOTIVATE

It is also very critical to properly motivate your team-mates. In a recent Gallop survey of employees, it was revealed that half were actually not mindfully engaged in their work.[16] Clearly the productivity of our workforce is reduced when people are distracted and not motivated to deliver excellent results.

A company will be most successful when the employees are actually thinking positively about their work. A great company doesn't just employ a body on the job. We must learn to utilize all of the talents of each employee. When people are bored or frustrated, Stinking Thinking will dominate their mindset. When facing daily frustrations, it's a natural human reaction to complain about anything and everything. And, when people are habitually complaining, they are not being productive!

I want to emphasize that positive motivation is primarily about the job, itself. Here is an awesome opportunity for Advanced Thought Planning.

As a leader ask yourself: What you can do to ensure that every job in your group is as stimulating as possible for that employee?

Make certain that the job and the employee are well matched to each other. For example, a quiet individual may not be the best person to select as a Walmart store greeter. Or, in the case of engineers, they usually prefer jobs that are more open ended in terms of technology.

Enlightened Thinking dictates that, whenever possible, let the employee help you define their job responsibilities.

When an employee is dissatisfied with their job, nothing you do will be effective in building a motivated employee, unless you change the job content.

Early in my career at Bell Labs we developed a bipolar microprocessor which used programmable read-only memories. Before the full manufacturing facility was available for our use, someone had to program these memories by hand. Initially it took many hours to manually set the switches to program all of the bits of a 64,000 bit chip. Of course, no one wanted to do this work for days and weeks at a time.

So, we turned the job into a competitive game! During lunch breaks we challenged fellow employees to set a new record in productivity and quality. The work became a highly motivational challenge to dozens of competitors. Through this competition, we improved the time to program a memory chip from six hours down to two hours. Fortunately the manufacturing facility was up and running before the competitive excitement wore off.

Today, many of our work responsibilities are actually team responsibilities. Teams of employees may need help to better relate to one another, and to better understand one another's expectations. Team building sessions that are focused on business goal definition and work methods can yield great team output. Personally I believe that the pure team building approach is a waste of time, if it only deals with personality traits. Always tie the team building sessions to your business goals.

Rewarding people for excellent work results is mandatory.

Thoroughly investigate salary structures in your industry and make sure that your company's salary structure is competitive. You want to ensure that your people believe that they are being treated fairly, and you also want to ensure that you can recruit excellent new hires when necessary. When people believe that they are not being treated fairly, the result is extensive Stinking Thinking on the job, which leads to a great deal of wasted time spent complaining around the water cooler.

At Xilinx each year, we would share salary survey results with similar technology companies. These anonymous surveys were then shared with all of our employees. The result was that people understood why there were certain salary increases set for that year. We tried to empower Enlightened Thinking to the greatest extent possible, by providing accurate competitive salary information. We also utilized a profit sharing program so everyone could benefit from the company's success.

Within your salary structure, you must ensure that the people who are most responsible for the company's success are rewarded at the highest level. I believe that the employees who contribute the most to success should receive the highest income. This seems obvious to most people, but I've been amazed at the number of times that, after checking, I've found great employees in the middle of the pay scale.

There had been many excuses offered to me as to why the excellent employees were not adequately compensated, but this is not a topic for Stinking Thinking! Excuses may be wide and varied, but these situations need to be rectified as quickly as possible. However, you must be careful about how you determine which employees are contributing the most to success.

It's very easy to conclude that a person who is solving many problems has contributed a great deal to the success of a project. But, be sure to check into who is responsible for originating those problems. If it's one and the same person, then this person may actually be responsible for delaying the project.

Always keep in mind that smart people solve problems, but the best people prevent problems.

It is always most effective to utilize a team approach when determining salaries and raises. There is a subtle form of Stinking Thinking that often impacts a manager. Sometimes the direct manager can be biased by a friendship that has developed at work, and as a result, they do not really perceive which employee is the highest contributor. Humanly speaking, it is very easy to become biased in favor of a friend, or someone whose style is like your own. A team of peer managers should be assembled annually to review salaries for their teams. Again, I want to emphasize, that it's critical that all employees believe that they are being fairly evaluated and compensated financially.

I also believe that employees should receive bonuses for contributions beyond the normal call of duty. Let's do some Advanced Thought Planning about this topic. How can we trigger Enlightened Thinking?

It's actually not about the amount of money that's granted to the employee, but the real advantage is in the recognition given with the bonus.

The recognition can either be given publicly or privately. It's about encouraging people when they do well. As a leader one of your key roles is to be an encourager. People just love to go home and share with their spouses about how they were given a special compliment from their manager. Often it's useful to give an employee or an entire team special recognition without any financial bonus.

During a team meeting, all you need to do is mention by name the person who performed at an exceptional level. Or, possibly send out an email that is complimentary of that person. That individual will feel very special and may even remember the occasion for many years. When people feel special, they enjoy coming into work each morning. They are much more likely to spend their time involved in Enlightened Thinking and productive work.

We humans do appreciate being appreciated. More than ten years ago I was speaking at a Mentor Graphics Corporation customer event. They sent a professional photographer to take my picture for the foyer at the conference center. After the event was concluded, they gave me the large printed picture. My wife still has that photograph of me in our family room. Because the photographer was truly professional, he took several hundred pictures. They printed the best one. It is the best picture of me that I have ever seen. I still have fond memories of working with Mentor Graphics! (OK; knock off the jokes. I don't know why it took hundreds of photos to get one good one.)

Anything that you can do that reduces the amount of complaining at work will improve overall productivity. When someone spends their time complaining, they are not spending their time getting work accomplished. And to make matters worse, they are also wasting the time of another employee who is listening to them complain. This is one of the reasons why layoffs are so damaging to productivity. The people who have not been released from the company will spend months and years complaining about the other people who were mistreated during the layoff, in their humble opinion.

Also, be very careful about distributing large executive bonuses which are not clearly linked to business goals. Certainly that type of compensation is not appropriate. Just ask your stockholders. In addition most employees will believe that these payouts are unfair, leading to a lot of complaining and wasted time on the job. Stinking Thinking will run rampant!

When tough times arrive in your industry or in the world, as is currently the case, treat employees with as much tender loving care as is possible. For example if the downturn appears to be temporary, it may be best to do pay reductions across the employee base before resorting to layoffs. I can recall about a decade ago at Xilinx, we announced that in order to avoid layoffs we would all receive a pay cut for several quarters. The executives actually received the largest percentage cuts in the company.

The amount of good will that was created with the employee base was astounding, and it persisted for many years. People felt that the management team had acted fairly, and they could be trusted to take the right action in the future. All of the employees felt that they were a team who could work together, and suffer together, in order to manage through the downturn. As a management team through Advanced Thought Planning we had created an environment of Enlightened Thinking.

Speaking of layoffs, as I have described, it is best to only do them when it is absolutely necessary. In today's business climate there is a great deal of Stinking Thinking around the topic of layoff programs. Many companies have used the poor economy as an excuse to justify layoffs, while their profitability is at an all-time high. In reality these companies use layoff programs to eliminate poor performing personnel.

However, these companies should invest the necessary resources to properly manage employee performance. A layoff program should not replace formal employee performance management.

Every employee should be coached by their manager, and they should be given accurate, timely feedback on their job performance. In addition, every employee deserves to receive a documented annual performance appraisal. If the employee is not contributing at minimum expectations for their job, after a period of time with coaching, they should be told that they will be dismissed in 30 days, unless a dramatic improvement occurs in their productivity. Most people in that situation will chose to leave the company of their own volition. If they do not leave and they do not improve their work output, then they should be dismissed quickly after the 30 days has elapsed. In my experience, it's actually better for that person to find a job through which they can perform well and be successful. We're not doing an employee a favor by letting them remain in a job in which they can't succeed. In addition, it's also better for the other employees on that team. Usually people know when a team member is not contributing at the appropriate level, and, they are often struggling to try to compensate for that team member by carrying an additional work load. Very quickly resentment can build and management is blamed for not taking the appropriate action.

In summary, proper overall motivation of people is crucial to your success as a leader. When people feel valued by the management team, they not only work harder, but they also work smarter. For example Wim Roelandts, our CEO at Xilinx, would often comment that he had never seen an engineer with low motivation create a great new idea. If you are expecting people to create new and better ideas, the work environment needs to be positive and uplifting. I would encourage you to spend a great deal of time in Advanced Thought Planning around this topic of motivation. The benefits you gain for your team will be enormous.

PROMOTIONS

Promotions of course can be very exciting and encouraging. Promotions are also crucial to the success of your company, so be very careful about how you determine who should be promoted into a particular position. Unconscious Stinking Thinking can lead you to promote a friend, or someone who you know has worked 'hard' for you. You may feel that you owe them the job. But, are they the best person for the job?

If you have an open position in your organization, Enlightened Thinking should lead you to write down the necessary qualifications and widely scan for potential candidates within your organization. In addition, speak with the team members about possible candidates. Speak with other managers in your company about additional candidates in other organizations.

Finally at this point, you are ready to start the interview process. Interviewers should include you, other managers, and a few of the team members. At the conclusion of the interviews collect all of the feedback and make a reasonably quick selection of a person for the promotion. It's best not to keep everyone in suspense for too long a period of time.

But if you can't find an excellent candidate within the company, then proceed to search for candidates with proper qualifications outside the company. You will do a terrible disservice to everyone on this team if you promote a current employee who is not appropriate for the job. You are also hurting that promoted employee, if they wind up failing on the job. You absolutely want to promote the best person available.

The bottom line is that promotions and hiring should be undertaken very seriously and conducted extremely well.

SOAR WITH EAGLES

Here is one last bit of Advanced Thought Planning on the topic of people as your most important asset: always spend your time on the job with the best people. If you are a great employee, you will surround yourself with other great employees. In hindsight, my most exciting years on the job were during the times that I had the privilege to be part of an awesome team of people.

Way back in the 1980's I was a manager at Bell Northern Research located in California. We were responsible for the product development of the office systems sold by Northern Telecom, the largest Canadian company at that time. These Meridian products became number one in the market around the world. We had a team of awesome hardware and software engineers. Everyone worked hard and the results were fantastic. We enjoyed each other's company so much that we even formed a softball team and joined the league in

Palo Alto, California. I would rather soar with eagles than struggle with failure.

However, sometimes human fear can cause us to indulge in Stinking Thinking. We too often worry that another great employee on the team may someday take our job away from us. Well, that may be true; but, that may also be the best outcome for your company. We need to focus our thinking around the best outcome for the team.

When you interview candidates for an open job, do you feel intimidated by strong candidates? Isn't that feeling of intimidation just more Stinking Thinking? Think about that self-talk. It really is best to be aggressive and consider who will replace you in your job someday. We need to realize that part of our job responsibility is to plan for our own replacement. You should always be doing succession planning together with your manager.

If your fear causes you to shun great people, then, you are not a great employee!

In that case it's time for you to improve yourself, and begin looking out for the best interests of your company. I'm quite sure that your manager will notice, and appreciate, your new attitude.

PERSONAL APPLICATION

1) How can I increase my contribution to this team?
2) Do I promote my friends over the best candidate?
3) Am I intimidated by strong employees?
4) Do I hire the best?
5) Write down your Big Decision:

<u>A COMPANY IS ONLY AS GOOD AS THE PEOPLE</u>

A COMPANY CAN ONLY IMPROVE IF THE PEOPLE IMPROVE

✳✳✳✳

I MUST IMPROVE

✳✳✳✳

MOTIVATION – IT'S ALL ABOUT THE JOB

✳✳✳✳

SMART PEOPLE SOLVE PROBLEMS GENIUSES PREVENT PROBLEMS

✳✳✳✳

ALWAYS ASSOCIATE WITH THE BEST PEOPLE

✳✳✳✳

ENCOURAGE PEOPLE – IT'S FREE

SELF-TALK on PEOPLE

ADVANCED THOUGHT PLANNING:

DO I APPRECIATE MY TEAM MEMBERS?

IS MY TEAM HIGHLY MOTIVATED?

AM I HIGHLY MOTIVATED?

****

THE BIG DECISION:

I WILL IMPROVE BY FOCUSING ON BUILDING PEOPLE

Chapter Eleven

Conclusion

—❦—

C onsistent with my intent to keep this book simple, I'd like to offer a brief conclusion by summarizing the key concepts presented in this book.

- ➤ Your self-talk will determine who you are in every aspect of your life.
- ➤ Take the time to do Advanced Thought Planning and become conscious of your Stinking Thinking, while you strive to maximize your Enlightened Thinking.
- ➤ Make the Big Decision to change your life habits, to be the best you can be.
- ➤ Choose one habit at a time to improve, for your betterment and the success of your company.
- ➤ Always live and work with integrity; be honest with yourself and all the people whom you impact on a daily basis.
- ➤ Keep in mind that your character is on display at all times.
- ➤ Be intelligently aggressive in everything you do; remember that without risk there is usually little to gain.

> ➤ Always keep your products and organization as simple as is possible; it really does make life easier to live.
> ➤ Focus is crucial to getting things done quickly and successfully; it's often necessary to say "no" to a myriad of distractions.
> ➤ In business and in life set goals that are measurable, so you can know for sure that you are making progress.
> ➤ Finally, always remember that people are your company's most valuable resource; and, that definitely includes you!

As you practice these principles, you will be actively building a culture for your company. It will be a culture of human respect, with a focus on delivering great results.

This is your life; think about it! I wish you success.

Appendix

Success According To God

—∞∞—

I'm a dedicated Christian. Jesus is my number one priority in life. I usually pray and read my Bible on a daily basis. Hence, many of you will likely conclude that I'm emotionally biased when it comes to the topic of God. But I'm not an emotional zealot; I'm logical and intellectual. How did I get to this point in my belief about God?

About 25 years ago I started to intensely analyze and investigate my beliefs about God. I did Advanced Thought Planning on the topic of faith. First I had to recognize my Stinking Thinking on this topic! Most of what the media has to say about faith is just nonsense. For example, in 2000, the ABC network broadcast a special hosted by the late Peter Jennings entitled *The Search for Jesus*. In 2004, Jennings hosted another documentary entitled *Jesus and Paul: The Word and the Witness*. These programs essentially asserted that the Bible was full of contradictions. But, they didn't offer a single example. They were very sloppy in their analysis, to say the least!

I spoke with numerous people with various opinions on faith, and I began to study the Bible. To make a very long story short, I made the Big Decision. I logically concluded that the Bible must have been inspired by God. God chose to tell us about himself through this book. Many people want to invent their own God, but God anticipated our arrogance and revealed himself to us.

It's basically impossible for a human to describe a God whom we have never directly encountered during our lives. But, that doesn't stop us from trying! Our minds are often filled with horrible misconceptions about God. Stinking Thinking about God is very common. What comes to your mind when you hear the word 'God?' Always keep in mind that we must know what we don't know, or we're dangerous.

However, God has made knowing himself easy, if we simply read the Bible. Enlightened Thinking should lead us to intensely study the relevant evidence.

I challenge you to put aside any Stinking Thinking about God, and do your own Advanced Thought Planning. This topic can have an impact upon you for all of eternity.

How do I know that I can believe the Bible? After 20-plus years of studying and teaching the Bible, I'm constantly amazed at the wisdom and consistency of this book. The Bible was written by 40-plus authors over a period of more than 1,500 years, and yet the Bible gives us a consistent description of God. From a human perspective, I can't even begin to imagine 40 authors writing in a consistent manner! God must have been providing the necessary guidance. In addition, archaeology has also confirmed a great deal of the content of the Bible as accurate.

Finally, the Bible contains hundreds of prophecies that have been fulfilled over these past thousands of years. So, based upon my intellectual analysis, I believe the Bible. If you are not sure for yourself, I'd also suggest that you read *The Case for Christ*, by Lee Strobel.[17] Strobel was an former award-winning legal editor of *The Chicago Tri-*

bune who conducted his own extensive investigation, just to prove to his wife that Christianity was false. It's interesting that his arrogant Stinking Thinking actually led him to do some serious Advanced Thought Planning.

Strobel concluded that in a court of law there is more than ample evidence to prove that the Bible is accurate, and that Jesus is God. His book is a thorough treatment of his investigation and decision to become a dedicated Christian. He is now one of the most popular Christian speakers in America, and around the world.

My God is Jesus. The Bible actually enables me to know Jesus through his words and actions. He loves me so much that he died on that cross for me, and for you. His death was necessary because, for the sake of justice, someone had to pay for my lying, cheating, stealing, and other sins. Only Jesus, who is God, could pay the price of the sins of billions of human beings. Now that my sins are paid for I have the free gift of heaven, because I have put my faith in Jesus and agreed to follow him.

You can be guaranteed of heaven as well, if you accept Jesus' death for your sins and agree to follow him.

If you really want to know Jesus, pray and ask him to reveal himself to you. Jesus wants to communicate with you as your God. The Bible clearly tells us that Jesus is God and the Savior of the world. If you want more information, please, check out the website www.meant4more.com, and watch the videos about what Jesus has to say in the Bible concerning his love for us.[18] You can also participate in the various chat rooms about the Christian faith.

The Bible also has a lot to say about how we should live and work. There are many great words of wisdom in the Bible! For example in the Bible the book of *Proverbs 1:5* (chapter one and verse five) says: "A wise man will hear and increase in learning." We should always get input from other people on the job if we want to learn.

Or, I also like the saying from the book of *Ecclesiastes 10:10* where it states: "A dull axe requires great strength, be wise and sharpen the blade." It always pays great rewards if we work smart, and hopefully avoid working long tiring hours.

The book of *Ecclesiastes 5:19* also states: "Moreover, when God gives any man wealth and possessions, and enables him to enjoy them, to accept his lot and be happy in his work—this is a gift of God."

JESUS ON FOCUS

Jesus knew exactly why he had come to planet earth as a human being. In the book of *John 18:37*, Jesus said: "In fact, for this reason I was born, and for this I came into the world, to testify to the truth." When you clearly know your objective and purpose, it enables you to focus. Jesus' whole life was dedicated to sharing critical truths.

In *Matthew 22:26* Jesus said: "What good will it be for a man if he gains the whole world, yet forfeits his soul?" On one occasion Jesus was asked which is the greatest commandment given by God. In *Matthew 22:27*, Jesus replied: "Love the Lord your God with all your heart and with all your soul and with all your mind."

On another occasion Jesus, as the merchant, told us how much he loved each one of us; he said in *Matthew 13:45*: "Again, the kingdom of heaven is like a merchant looking for fine pearls. When he found one of great value, he went away and sold everything he had and bought it."

Jesus' focus was to tell us that our focus needs to be on God, and obeying his loving directions. In *Matthew 9:35* the Bible says: "Jesus went through all of the towns and villages, teaching in their synagogues, preaching the good news of the kingdom." In *Matthew 6:24* Jesus did have a serious warning for us about focus: "No one can serve two masters. Either he will hate the one and love the other, or he will be devoted to the one and despise the other. You cannot serve both God and money."

Jesus specializes in Enlightened Thinking! He was not saying that money is evil, but rather that it is simply less important than God. In *Matthew 6:23* Jesus said: "But seek first His kingdom and righteousness, and all these things will be given to you as well." Jesus of course knew human nature, and He knew that many of us would not want to listen to His message.

In *Matthew 10:14,* He said to His followers: "If anyone will not welcome you or listen to your words, shake off the dust from your feet when you leave that home or town." Jesus was telling His followers that it was their focus to go out and share the truths about God. But, if some people would not listen to the truth, then they needed to leave and find another home where they were welcome. God created human beings with free will. He will not force us to focus on Him and live in a close relationship with Him. But, God does want everyone to hear the truth and make a decision about Him. God does want us to do some intense Advanced Thought Planning about our future with Him.

PAUL ON SELF-TALK

In the book of *Second Corinthians*, the author, the Apostle Paul, actually has a lot to say about self-talk. In Chapter Ten there is a discussion about the importance of taking every one of our thoughts captive and not just idly letting our minds wander aimlessly: "…we take captive every thought to make it obedient to Christ." We are encouraged to analyze our thoughts, and focus on the thoughts that are good and pleasing to God. Of course, it goes without saying that the thoughts which are pleasing to God are also what are best for us!

In *Ephesians 4:22* Paul observes that if we are to turn off bad thoughts then we must turn on good thoughts: "put off your old self...be made new in the attitude of your minds...put on the new self, created to be like God in true righteousness." It is exactly from this verse that I decided that Enlightened Thinking is to be maximized and Stinking Thinking is to be minimized. Our minds are very interesting and complicated 'computers;' it's nearly impossible for us to think about nothing. Go ahead right now, try to think about nothing. I will wager that you will not be able to do it for more than a few seconds.

So, we must purposefully fill our minds with good thoughts, Enlightened Thinking, or else our minds will be filled with random garbage, Stinking Thinking.

In *Philippians 4:8* Paul says "...whatever is true, whatever is noble, whatever is right...if anything is excellent... think about such things." In *Romans 12:3* Paul says: "Do not think of yourself more highly than you ought, but rather think of yourself with sober judgment."

Our pride begins with our Stinking Thinking. We need to minimize the time we spend thinking about ourselves, and when we do think about ourselves, we need to try and perceive ourselves as objectively as possible. It is virtually impossible to be objective about myself! I can't really see myself from a distance; I'm very biased. So, I do need to be conscious of these thoughts whenever I do get focused on myself. Am I using sober judgment in my self-assessment?

In *Colossians 3:2* Paul tells us to "set your mind on things above." Let's not dwell upon ourselves too long. In summary, Paul certainly understood that how we think is crucial to who we are and how we behave. In the Bible Paul is not the only person whom God has used to speak to us about self-talk. For example in *Proverbs 23:7* Solomon says "as a man thinks...so he is." In *Second Peter 3:1* Peter says "I have written...to stimulate you to wholesome thinking." And as a final example of God's concern for 'how' we think, in the book of *Matthew 6:34* Jesus says "Therefore do not worry about tomorrow, for tomorrow will worry about itself. Each day has enough trouble of its own."

NEHEMIAH ON WORK

One of my favorite books in the Bible dealing with the topic of work is *Nehemiah*. He was employed as a high official in the court of the king of Babylon when he heard about the plight of the Jews in the conquered city of Jerusalem. Let's take a look at how Nehemiah lived out our various management principles for success.

Nehemiah was a man of great integrity. For example he honestly told the king that he wanted to go to Jerusalem to rebuild the city. He knew that the king could literally take off his head for such an unanticipated request. Nehemiah was afraid of what the king might do to him. But despite his fears, Stinking Thinking which we all have from time to time, Nehemiah spoke truth to the king in a straightforward manner. Nehemiah spent many weeks in Advanced Thought Planning through prayer. He conquered his fear by planning his discussion with the king. This example is exactly how we should relate to our manager at work.

Nehemiah's character is clearly on display as he interacts with the various people on the job. He was a man of humility. When he first arrived in Jerusalem, he kept a low profile. He took the time to do his Advanced Thought Planning. He then asked the people what they needed, and how he should proceed with the rebuilding plans. He was friendly and open with his fellow workers. He communicated his decisions and plans in a clear manner. When he was questioned by the people, he gave them more details. When troubles arose on the job, he quickly addressed the issues. He stopped any Stinking Thinking as quickly as possible. He often was working side by side with other team members, so he understood the issues clearly. With his enemies he was tough and unwavering. Even they had a great deal of respect for Nehemiah.

I believe that Nehemiah's middle name should have been 'Aggressive.' He wanted to rebuild the city walls as quickly as possible for protection against possible attacks. When some of his fellow workers were lazy on the job, he confronted them outwardly. And Nehemiah was a man who specialized in Enlightened Thinking. He did not over extend his team during the work. He made sure that they had the resources necessary to finish the job. He also knew what he didn't know. When he first arrived in the city, he quietly went out to survey the demolished city walls. It was only after that fact finding trip that he formulated his plans for the work ahead.

Nehemiah managed to keep his project as simple as possible. His organization structure was very straightforward. Families were assigned to rebuild the part of the city wall that was right next to their homes. People were very motivated to protect their homes and families. Everyone had a clear job responsibility.

Nehemiah's focus was like a laser. When his enemies called upon him for a series of meetings, he said: "no." He said that he was too busy to be attending pointless meetings. That philosophy sounds perfect to me!

Nehemiah did his measuring by MBWA (management by walking around). He could readily see how high the wall was progressing in different parts of the city. Even more important, he was able to talk with people and assess their morale. He also periodically called meetings with his leaders to get their accurate reports. When there were issues identified in these reports, Nehemiah took decisive action.

Nehemiah knew that the people were his best asset. When some of the people fell down on the job, he tried to lift them up with consistent encouragement. In a few cases for the sake of the greater good of the people, he fired several leaders. When these leaders failed him, he conducted a public confrontation. It was clear to the workers that these few leaders had let them down, and action was necessary. Nehemiah was an effective thoughtful leader.

Finally, and most important, Nehemiah was a prayer warrior. He knew that without God the work was doomed to failure. Even Jesus, who is God, prayed regularly. In the book of *Mark 1:35* it says: "Very early in the morning, while it was still dark, Jesus got up, left the house and went off to a solitary place, where he prayed."

So for those of you who are Christian, I'd like to add one more key management principle: prayer.

I have found that prayer consistently stops Stinking Thinking and initiates Enlightened Thinking. My wife and I start most mornings with a time of prayer. I simply ask God for His guidance and wisdom in my life. I ask God to lead me in His direction, according to His will for me. If there is something that I want, I ask God to 'close doors' and block me, if it's not His will for my life. It's very reassuring to know that if I'm in God's will, then He is on my side. Or, I should say that I'm on His side. The bottom line is that I know that my God is far wiser than myself, and letting Him control my decisions will lead to far better results for me. It gives me great confidence and peace to walk with my almighty God.

This is the ultimate form of Advanced Thought Planning: ask God, who is all wise, to guide you according to His purposes.

PROVERBS ON LIFE

The book of *Proverbs* is full of hundreds of great words of wisdom for life. I'd like to quote several of them that apply especially well to a work situation.

Integrity:
The man of integrity walks securely. (*10:9*)
Do not accuse a man for no reason when he has done you no harm. (*3:30*)
Ill-gotten treasures are of no value. (*10:2*)
An evil man is trapped by his sinful talk. (*12:13*)
Kings take pleasure in honest lips; they value a man who speaks the truth. (*16:13*)

Humility:
Do you see a man wise in his own eyes? There is more hope for a fool than for him. (*26:12*)
Discretion will protect you, and understanding will guard you. (*2:11*)
He mocks proud mockers but gives grace to the humble. (*3:34*)
A fool shows his annoyance at once, but a prudent man overlooks an insult. (*12:16*)

Be Aggressive:
Wisdom is supreme; therefore get wisdom. Though it cost you all you have, get understanding. (*4:7*)
Whoever ignores correction leads others astray. (*10:17*)
It is not good to have zeal without knowledge. (*19:2*)

Keep It Simple:
A man of understanding keeps a straight course. (*15:21*)

Focus:
Let your eyes look straight ahead, fix your gaze directly before you. (*4:25*)
A discerning man keeps wisdom in view, but a fool's eyes wander to the ends of the earth. (*17:24*)
He who works his land will have abundant food, but he who chases fantasies lacks judgment. (*12:11*)

Measure It:
The plans of the diligent lead to profit as surely as haste leads to poverty. (*21:5*)
A simple man believes anything, but a prudent man gives thought to his steps. (*14:15*)
He who hates correction is stupid. (*12:1*)
The first to present his case seems right, till another comes forward and questions him. (*18:17*)

People:
He who walks with the wise grows wise, but a companion of fools suffers harm. (*13:20*)
Of what use is money in the hand of a fool, since he has no desire to get wisdom. (*17:16*)
Do not withhold good from those who deserve it, when it is in your power to act. (*3:27*)
Rebuke a wise man and he will love you. (*9:8*)
Honor the Lord with your wealth...then your barns will be overflowing... (*3:9*)

WHAT REALLY MATTERS IN LIFE

I have great peace. People who know me well often wonder how it is that I can be calm in the midst of a storm.

One of my great strengths is the ability to be in a meeting discussing some huge business failing without getting very emotional. Sometimes I'm even amazed at the non-anxious presence that I possess! I guess that I'm just amazing !

No, I'm not that wonderful. Let's do a little Advanced Thought Planning to prove it. I believe that when I die, after a few or many more years of life, that I will be with Jesus in heaven for eternity. And, I know that eternity is a very long time to be in heaven, compared to my relatively short life on earth. I also know that Jesus will reward us for the works that we performed on earth in obedience to him.

So, let's imagine that I'm in a meeting and our project milestones are in real jeopardy. As the manager, I can feel very embarrassed at our obvious, imminent failure. The presentation is looking very pathetic and everyone is feeling defeated. This is serious business! My reaction is to focus on the needed plans to rectify this project.

If I'm tempted to get emotional, I simply recall that this too 'will pass.' I have already made my Big Decision: this project does not define my self-worth. I focus my self-talk on Enlightened Thinking: how can we succeed? I know that I am a child of God. I know that I have tried to do the best possible job for my company. I do not fear the earthly consequences of a failed project. And, I certainly don't start thinking about exaggerated negative outcomes.

If I'm tempted to get into Stinking Thinking, I put on the thought that I know that I know that Jesus loves me. The Bible says "...if God be for me, who can be against me." All of this self-talk happens in a few seconds, and it may get repeated many times during the course of this meeting. As a result, I can be non-anxious and focused on success: how we will resolve the issues with this project.

All of this Enlightened Thinking is possible because of Jesus. It is not me. I simply know that I have an awesome

God, who has great plans for me now and through eternity. And, the good news is that this same God loves you as well!

Seriously consider committing your life to Jesus. You have nothing to lose and everything to gain.

Notes

⸻

[1] Karlgaard, Rich. *Forbes* magazine editorial; February 28, 2011.

[2] O'Neil, William J. *How to Make Money in Stocks*; 2011.

[3] *Forbes* magazine editorial; February, 2009.

[4] Preston, Rob. *Information Week* editorial; November 24, 2008.

[5] Ariely, Dan. *Predictably Irrational*; 2008.

[6] Sager, Ryan. *SmartMoney* magazine; December, 2010.

[7] Sager, Ryan. *SmartMoney* magazine; December, 2010.

[8] Johnson, Paul. *Forbes* magazine; December 6, 2010.

[9] Kern, Frank. *Business Week*; May 19, 2010.

[10] Stone, Douglas. *Difficult Conversations*; 1999.

[11] DeMarco, Tom. *Peopleware*; 1987.

[12] *San Francisco Chronicle*; June 23, 2011.

[13] Columbia Accident Investigation Board Report Volume 1; August, 2003.

[14] *InformationWeek*; Dr. Dobbs Report; September, 2009.

[15] DeMarco, Tom. *Peopleware*; 1987.

[16] Burger, Arlen. *Leadership News Letter*; July, 2009.

[17] Strobel, Lee. *The Case for Christ*; 1998.

[18] www.meant4more.com; Website owned by Global Media Outreach.

About The Author

────── ⚬⚭⚬ ──────

R ichard Sevcik was born in Chicago. He's the product of a strong Catholic elementary and high school training. Rich graduated as a James Scholar, Magna Cum Laude from the University of Illinois, BS in Engineering Physics with a major in mathematics. He was granted his Master's Degree in Electrical Engineering from Northwestern University. Rich was employed for 10 years at AT&T, Bell Laboratories. He worked as a circuit designer and software engineer. He participated in the first cell phone trial in Oak Park, Illinois. Rich then moved to California and joined Bell Northern Research, Northern Telecom. As a vice president he led the development of the Meridian Office Communication System, which achieved number one market share during the 1980's. After eight years Rich joined Hewlett Packard's computer group. Again as vice president, group general manager he led a team of 2,000 engineers in the development of HP's computer servers, workstations, and networking systems. HP's compute servers still enjoy a number one market share worldwide. Finally after 10 years Rich joined Xilinx, Inc. in the programmable logic industry. As executive vice president he led the development of the Xilinx ISE customer software tools, plus the Virtex and Spartan semiconductor product lines. Both of these product lines became number one in market share with the company exceeding $1.7 billion in revenue with more than 25 percent net income.

Currently Rich is retired from full time employment. He does consulting work part time, including two board seats. Rich and his wife also lead a Christian ministry called God Talk, speaking with un-churched people about God at local retail malls. (For more information, see www.Godtalkinthe-mall.com.)